A STAR FOR STELLA

DREAM BIG!

Julia Baez

A STAR FOR STELLA

A MOTHER'S JOURNEY TO OVERCOME

LEIA BAEZ

NEW DEGREE PRESS

A STAR FOR STELLA
A Mother's Journey to Overcome

ISBN   978-1-63730-709-0   Paperback
            978-1-63730-847-9   Kindle Ebook
            979-8-88504-006-8   Ebook

DISCLAIMER
The names of some individuals in this memoir have been changed to respect their privacy.

To my Estella,
for always reminding me to look for the rainbow after
it rains and to search for the stars on the darkest of
nights. You will forever be my greatest blessing.

CONTENTS

"I now see how owning our story and loving ourselves through that process is the bravest thing that we will ever do."

—BRENÉ BROWN

AUTHOR'S NOTE

—

Fifty thousand…sixty thousand…three hundred fifty thousand…one million! Just a few days after my commencement speech video was shared online by the media company Goalcast, more than three million people around the world had listened to me openly share the darkest, most difficult times in my life. Day by day, minute by minute, the number of people who were moved by my message kept climbing. The number of likes, comments, and shares kept ticking upward, too.

I had to pick up my jaw from the floor. I couldn't believe this was happening. It was so bizarre to see *my story* on YouTube reaching more than 6.5 million people across the globe and having such a positive impact.

The social media notifications kept lighting up. I had messages on Facebook from women and men from all over the world—Australia, India, England, Canada, Jamaica, New Jersey, Texas—thanking me for courageously sharing my story of overcoming a painful divorce and custody battle and giving them a sense of hope. Their encouraging messages saying my speech was "incredibly powerful," "inspiring," and "motivating" really lifted me up.

I had friend requests from complete strangers. Alyzabeth Paul from Houston, Texas, was one of them. She said she was compelled to connect with me on Facebook because she wanted me to know just how meaningful my words were for her. In a Facebook message, she wrote, "Thank you for being the one to push me when times get rough. I was in a moment of being overwhelmed when I saw your speech! Needless to say, God spoke through you. Thank you!"

Her words instantly brought me to tears. I felt so much peace in that moment because I, too, felt like God was using me as a vessel. I thought to myself, *Wow! Maybe this has been God's plan all along. Maybe there is purpose for pain. Maybe I am right where I am supposed to be, sharing my journey to lift others up.*

My cellphone wouldn't stop buzzing with text messages from friends and family:

"Are you seeing this? 6.5 million views. You are a viral superstar!"

"OMG, You are amazing. Can I have your autograph?"

"You are worldwide, cuz! Keep shining!"

I had experienced the power of storytelling many times before in my over fourteen years as an award-winning newspaper journalist. I saw firsthand how stories can magically connect, inspire, and uplift people with all different beliefs and backgrounds. But January 27, 2018, was the first time in my life I had ever publicly shared a piece of my own story, not to mention on a stage in front of hundreds of people. I was graduating with my master's degree from Bellevue University. I was thirty-five years old, but I was as nervous as a new kid on the first day of school when I hit that spotlight. My commencement speech marked the first time in my life I had dug up enough courage to be vulnerable and pour out my heart in hopes of inspiring just one person.

It worked, and not with just one person, but with millions. That was the evidence I needed to show I could be brave and share my story, regardless of what people might think. That was proof that on the other side of my fear was something truly remarkable: the opportunity to inspire so many people to keep going.

That's exactly why I continue to open up. That's why I wrote this book. I believe I step into my power every time I find the courage to share a piece of my journey. I know it in my heart that God is using my story to show others what is possible when you believe in yourself, have faith, and never give up.

By digging deep and being authentic, I was able to make an overwhelmingly positive impact on so many people—even complete strangers. I am hopeful *A Star for Stella* will do the same.

People related to my story because I wasn't afraid to show my messy side. For me, it was all about embracing my true self, the imperfectly perfect Chicana from Omaha, Nebraska, who wears her scars and flaws as badges of honor. This strong South Omaha girl stays determined to fly even when her wings need work. Something truly magical happens when you're brave enough to own your shit. People flock to that.

So, I'm bringing the realness with *A Star for Stella*. This book will take you through my journey to overcome a variety of personal battles. It's a story of self-discovery, shining a light on trauma, alcoholism, and divorce. It's my fight to be the best version of me so I can be the best mother possible.

I never imagined in a million years I would have to prove in a court of law I am worthy to be a mother. One tragic night sent my life spiraling out of control and my heart crashing into pieces.

When a judge decided to take my daughter away from me—my beautiful, fun-loving, energetic Stella—I felt like my life was over. It was the most soul-crushing news I could ever receive. While this story will take you to my ultimate lows, it will also lift you so much higher with hope and resilience.

After my commencement speech went viral, I was sought out to speak at a variety of events and conferences. It was through some of the most difficult times in my life I discovered my true passion for motivational speaking. I even landed a speaking gig at a women's leadership conference in London. I remember thinking, *How cool is this, I get paid to speak at events? What an awesome gig!*

At the same time, I still wasn't entirely proud of the life I was living because I was still struggling with a longtime addiction to alcohol. I was drinking to mask emotions I should have been working to heal. I know there are a lot of overwhelmed mamas and women—especially in this post-pandemic life—who can relate to this, so this book is for you. It's for anyone who needs an infusion of hope and to see how bad things can be used for good.

I believe this book will help you wherever you are in your journey and be the motivation you need to keep going. I hope it will lead you to the next step in your own journey of being the best version of yourself. When you have the courage to face whatever is holding you back, that's where you learn, grow, and level up.

Even though I often fall short, my goal has always been to be the best role model for my daughter, and writing *A Star for Stella* is a part of that ambition. I want Estella to see life isn't about being flawless. It's about falling and rising stronger. It's about making mistakes and learning and growing from them. It's about accepting our battles and embracing the lessons they bring.

I'm also writing this book for my family, a.k.a. Los Baez, who have always loved me unconditionally and continuously lift me up when I need it most. I want my niece and nephews to see anything is possible when you believe in your dreams. I want my parents to know they are my angels on Earth, and I am forever grateful for their unshakeable support. They are truly my best friends forever.

I've learned to stop questioning why certain things happen in life. I've experienced how the most terrible things can actually redirect us to the best things that will ever happen in our lives. This book is a testimony to that. My darkest times brought me to some of my brightest days, and my most heartbreaking struggles forced me to heal and grow in unimaginable ways. I'm finally on my way to meeting the best version of me, and I couldn't be more excited. I deserve to know her. We all deserve to know our best selves. Embrace your journey and trust you are right where you are supposed to be.

CHAPTER 1

IMPOSSIBLE TO FORGET

——

I woke up on the living room couch with my head spinning.

I could faintly hear my husband Jesse's voice from the kitchen.

"Good morning. How are you feeling?" he asked in his typical morning-person, cheerful tone.

"Uggghhh!" I said as I forced myself to sit up on the couch. "I feel awful *and* weird."

I looked down, surprised to see I was still wearing the clothes I had on the day before. That's odd. I hate sleeping in my bra.

Jesse kept talking to me despite my confusion. "I'm going to pick up Stella. Call your cousin Kerry and let her know I'm on my way."

"Okay," I mumbled as I started scanning the living room for my cellphone.

I was no stranger to a brutal hangover. I had plenty of mornings where I swore I would never drink alcohol again, but this felt different. Everything seemed so blurry. My brain felt foggy. My body felt weak. *What was wrong with me?* It was unlike me to pass out on the living room couch still wearing my clothes and my makeup from the night before. On top of that, how did I fall asleep with my contact lenses still in my eyes? I had to practically peel one eye open at a time because they were so dry and were nearly stuck shut. I never slept with my contacts in, even on my drunkest nights. *What was going on?*

I started to think back to the night before, but it felt impossible. Everything seemed unclear. *What even happened last night?* I remembered dropping my four-year-old daughter, Stella, off at my cousin Kerry's house a few blocks away so she could babysit while I met up with friends. Jesse was also going out with his coworkers, which is why we decided on a babysitter.

I picked up my cellphone and called my cousin so I could let her know Jesse was on his way.

Kerry's voice answered with laughter in it, "Hello."

I took a deep breath and tried to pull out my contact lens, which shot pain through my eyeball. "Hey, Jesse is coming to pick up Stella."

Kerry paused and then screamed in disbelief, "Shut up!"

I continued looking at myself in the bathroom mirror, trying to get my contact unstuck from my eye. "What?"

"Are you kidding me?" Kerry's voice raised a notch. "You picked her up last night!"

My knees started to tremble, and I lost my balance, falling onto the top of the toilet seat. "What?" I shouted.

Kerry was yelling at me now. "You don't remember? Where is she?"

I shot up off the toilet seat and grabbed the door jamb to get my balance. "Oh my God! *Stella*! I have to go, Kerry!"

I heard Kerry yell as I stood paralyzed in shock. "Call me back!"

In a frenzy, I immediately hung up the phone and started searching the entire house for my daughter. "Stella! Stella!

Stella!" I screamed as I frantically ran from room to room in the house. *Where was my baby? Why couldn't I remember picking her up last night? What happened to me?* I felt like everything around me just stopped. I couldn't even catch my breath.

My heart was racing, and I had this weird lump-in-my-throat feeling. I was scared shitless. *Where could my baby be?*

All I could do was cry. I was a mess. I was still running around the house and hoping she was playing hide-and-seek with me like we always did. I kept screaming for her. I ran outside of the house to retrace my steps. The bright sun hit me like a ton of bricks. I had to shield my eyes with my hand, especially because my contacts were still burning my eyes. *What was wrong with me?* I planned to run the perimeter of the house to see if she was outside somewhere, but for some reason my eyes were fixated on my white SUV. Something urged me to look inside. My intuition—a gut feeling, whatever it was—pushed me back into the house to grab my key fob before sprinting back outside. I hit the button and opened up the door. There she was, my Stella, still in the car and still buckled into her car seat. Her eyes were puffy from crying. Her pants were soiled with urine. It was the dead of summer, July 18, 2015.

What had I done? I quickly unbuckled her out of her car seat and hugged her so tight. "Hi, mamas! I am so sorry, baby. Are you okay?"

She looked up at me with worry still gripping her big, brown eyes as she said softly, "Mommy, you forgot me!"

I broke down in tears and squeezed her even tighter. "I am so sorry, baby!"

All sorts of thoughts ran through my mind. *Stella could have died. Someone could have kidnapped her. My baby could have died!* I was so thankful to God my daughter was awake, breathing, and alive, but I couldn't stop thinking about the terrible things that could have happened to her. It would have been all my fault. I was devastated.

Holding Stella tight at my hip, I quickly ran back into the house. I filled her sippy cup with water and took her straight into the bathroom. I removed all of her clothes to check her body and make sure she was all right. I put her in the bathtub to clean her up, and I couldn't control the tears streaming down my face. I thought to myself as I started cleaning her little body, *I am supposed to be her protector. I am supposed to keep her safe. How could I let this happen?* I was so angry with myself, but at the same time I was flustered because I didn't know what had happened to me. I tried to hide my tears from Stella because I didn't want to scare her more. My poor baby was traumatized at the hands of her own mother, and I could feel the shame pumping through my entire body.

I felt like everything I was doing was in slow motion. My brain was in a haze. I started praying in my head. *Lord God, I don't know what happened to me, but please let my baby be okay. Please let us both be okay.* I just couldn't stop thinking about how this could happen to me—and especially to my Stella. I was so scared.

I had so many questions and no answers. *How could I leave my daughter in the car overnight?*

I continued to bathe her and watch her closely as she started playing with her bath toys like normal and splashing around, being silly. While I was grateful she was unharmed, I couldn't help but think about how I could have let this happen. I couldn't help but try to piece together the night before in my head. I remember meeting my friend Daniel for pizza and appetizers around 7:00 p.m. and then heading to our friend Megan's going-away party afterward. I didn't plan on drinking much because I was driving, and I was intentionally trying to slow down on boozing anyway. It was getting in the way of my fitness goals and causing problems in my marriage. I planned to stick to beer so I could drive home safely and call it a night. I even turned down shots of tequila at the party because I wanted to be responsible. I was also afraid of getting a DUI and potentially ruining my career as a journalist.

I had a few beers with dinner and a few beers at the party—no more than five beers total over the course of five hours, and that was with a big dinner. Normally, that wouldn't even faze me. I was a heavy drinker, and I could handle my booze. So, blacking out and not remembering anything didn't add up. I knew something wasn't right.

Daniel and I had decided to leave the party about midnight. We left at the same time and walked out together. I felt fine. We talked and laughed as we walked to the parking lot to our cars. We said our goodbyes and drove off separately.

As I grabbed Stella out of the bathtub, I decided to get Daniel on the phone right away before Jesse got home. I wanted to see if there was more to the story. I was anxious to hear what he had to say because I wanted to make sense of this.

"What's up, what's up?" Daniel said. He was energetic and full of life—like always.

The tone in my voice was a dead giveaway something was wrong. "Was I drunk last night when we left the party? I need you to help me retrace my steps. Something terrible has happened and—"

Daniel interrupted me before I could say anything else. "Whoa, whoa, whoa, slow down! You're talking so fast I can barely understand you. Are you good?"

I snapped back at him, "No! I'm not! Was I drunk when we left Megan's party?"

Daniel was definitely concerned now because his voice was trembling. "No, you weren't drunk. I wouldn't let you drive home if you were drunk. We both had a few beers at Megan's. What happened? What's going on?"

I was emotional and could barely mumble my words through the crying and deep breaths. "I don't know what happened, but I somehow forgot Stella in the car overnight, and I don't remember anything."

"Holy shit," Daniel yelled. "Is Stella okay?"

"Yes, she's fine, thank God, but I am sure she's still scared," I wailed. "I feel horrible, and I don't understand any of this. Jesse is going to be home any minute so I have to go. Pray for me."

"Of course. Everything is going to be okay. Call me back!" Daniel was one of my best friends, and even in the hardest, most difficult situations, he always told me everything would work out. This time was different. I felt so uneasy, and I knew this wasn't going to go over well with Jesse. He had a temper and definitely hated my drinking. *There is no way this was going to work out for me.*

I heard Jesse open the front door. He started talking to me as he walked toward the bathroom, where I was drying Stella off. "Babe, your cousin wasn't home. No one answered the door." He walked into the bathroom and saw me holding Stella wrapped in a towel as I continued to cry. He looked at me confused. "What's going on? What happened?"

I hugged Stella closer to me. "I somehow left Stella in the car overnight. I dunno what happened. I'm scared. I don't feel right. Maybe I should go to the hospital."

Jesse lunged forward. *"What the fuck! Oh my god!"* He quickly grabbed Stella from my arms. "Are you okay, mamas?" he said to Stella as he hugged her.

Stella looked at her dad and hugged him again. She didn't have to say anything, but I knew she was scared and also relieved to be back in her parents' arms.

Jesse turned his head at me and glared. "You're a drunk. You're a stupid drunk!"

I put my hands up, reaching for Stella. "I wasn't drunk. I swear I wasn't drunk. Jesse, please believe me. Something happened. I think I was roofied or drugged. I've never felt like this before."

Jesse slapped my hands away. "Get out of my face. You're such a liar. You weren't drugged. You're a drunk."

"I wouldn't have driven home if I was drunk. You know that! Please listen to me. Something happened to me!"

Jesse was stubborn. There was no way he would ever believe me. I didn't exactly have the best track record when it came to alcohol, either. I liked to drink on a weekly basis, and a lot of the time it was to the point of being drunk. I hate to admit this, but I didn't have an off button. I always wanted the party to continue. I knew nothing about moderation, so Jesse had good reason not to believe me, even though this time I knew I wasn't drunk.

But it didn't matter. Jesse wouldn't talk to me. He wouldn't even look at me. Instead of helping me figure out what happened, like I wanted my husband to do, he made me feel like a monster and a careless mother who would intentionally hurt her child. I thought about going to the hospital to get checked out, but I became so focused on trying to get my husband to believe me and listen to me that I never went.

I had no clue what happened, and I felt so alone. I had this eerie feeling inside of my body. My stomach was in knots. I wanted it all to be a bad dream. I had so much anxiety, my legs wouldn't stop shaking. It kept replaying in my head: opening the door to find Stella in her car seat and the worry all over her adorable little face.

I could just see the headline now: "Drunk Mom Leaves Toddler in Car Overnight in Summer Heat." Those were always the kind of news stories that made me gasp. I had been a newspaper reporter for more than fourteen years, covering courts and crime and breaking news. I read through police reports and court affidavits and combed through extremely graphic details of cases. Anytime I would see a report of child abuse or child neglect, my heart would break, even more so after I became a mother myself.

Then it became my story, my headline. *Was I the drunk mom who left her kid in the car?*

I felt so small—like such a terrible person. Even if I was roofied, I still made the choice to drink alcohol that night, and that was weighing on me heavily. I knew I messed up, and I had a feeling in my gut. My life was about to change forever.

CHAPTER 2

RUNNING FROM REGRET

———

I still needed answers, so I called my cousin Kerry back since she would have seen me when I picked up Stella.

Kerry answered on the first ring, as if she were waiting by the phone for my call. "What is going on?"

I took a deep breath and got straight to the point. "I somehow left her in the car overnight. I barely remember being at your house to pick her up. What can you tell me?"

Kerry paused for a second. "Well, I was half-asleep when I heard you knocking at the door. I thought Stella was spending the night. You seemed tipsy, and I told you she could stay over, but you were adamant about taking her home. I told you to come back in the morning, but you refused."

I shook my head in disbelief. My hand was on my forehead and my fingers were rubbing at my temples. I had one of those painful headaches from crying. "I am so sorry! I don't remember feeling tipsy or even talking to you. My mind is messed up. Everything is a blur. I'm so sorry."

"Is Stella all right?" Kerry asked with concern in her voice.

"Yes! Thank God!" I exclaimed. "But I'm not. Jesse wants nothing to do with me. He's downstairs with Stella right now. I don't feel good about this."

"Wow! I'm sorry," Kerry said. She knew Jesse well, and she knew me even better. She knew our relationship was rocky, and I could hear the uneasiness in her voice.

The last thing I wanted was for her to feel guilty. This was all me. I raised my voice and said, "No, I'm sorry. I should have left her at your house. I have never felt like this after drinking. I'm so sure I was roofied, but Jesse doesn't believe me. Was I acting weird?"

Kerry took a second to think. "I mean, I was half-asleep. I didn't want you to take her."

I started to tremble. "Damn it! I am so sorry for putting you in this situation. I will call you later. Love you."

Kerry lived only a few blocks from me, but from the time I left the party to the time I got to her house—normally a fifteen-minute drive—I had no memory. It was gone.

My head collapsed into my hands after I hung up the phone with her. I couldn't stop sobbing.

I needed my parents. I told Jesse I was leaving to talk to them. He stayed with Stella at our house, but he still wasn't talking to me. I needed to talk to my number one supporters who weren't afraid to give me tough love. They lived about a ten-minute drive away from me, but I took the longer route to their house. I needed time to think. *How was I going to tell my parents what I had done?* I knew how disappointed they would be.

And I was right.

My father's words stung. He didn't even look at me when, in a stern voice, he said, "You messed up royally!"

I had nothing to say because I knew he was right, but I had to tell both my mom and dad because I was scared. I felt lost and full of uncertainty. My father didn't have anything else to say to me while I was there. His silence always had a way of saying so much more than his words ever could. I knew he was extremely upset. My mother, on the other hand, had a lot of questions. We sat down on the couch to talk.

I could see the distress in Mom's eyes before she even opened her mouth. "Are you sure Stella is going to be all right?" I nodded my head. I felt so defeated. "Physically, she's fine, but I don't know what this will do to her mentally. I mean, can you imagine how scared she must have been waking up in the car alone? Ugh! I get sick to my stomach just thinking about it."

She shook her head in disbelief. I could sense my mom's sorrow just sitting next to her. I knew she was worried about her Stella Bella.

"Where did you even go last night?" she asked.

"I met up with Daniel for pizza, and then we went to a friend's going-away party at an apartment complex."

My mom put her hand on my shoulder as I shared more details—the ones I could remember—because she could see my eyes welling up.

"How much did you drink?" she asked.

"That's just it, Mom. I was purposely not drinking a lot because I had to drive. I had two drinks at dinner, and I ate a lot. I even turned down shots at the party because I was sticking to beer. I thought I was acting responsibly."

My mom let out a big sigh and continued to console me, rubbing my back. "Maybe your body had a reaction to the alcohol. You have to slow down, Leia. You are lucky Stella didn't get hurt. Your guardian angel was with you both."

Every time my mom talks in a religious or spiritual manner, I get emotional. My mom has always been so spiritually intuitive, and it just reminds me of how lucky I am to have a strong faith and a foundation of love and support from my parents. This time, though, I just felt like a disappointment. *Would God ever forgive me?*

I hugged my mom and held her for a few minutes. It was comforting, and I could feel my anxiety going down the longer I held her warm, petite body. I looked at her and said, "Do you think I should go to the hospital? Could I have had a medical episode of some kind?"

She shook her head, unsure. "I don't know. Maybe someone put something in your drink at that party? Did you know all of the people there?"

My eyes lit up. My gut was telling me this was on target. "That's exactly what I was thinking, but I am not sure. I told Jesse that, but he didn't believe me, Mom."

She responded quickly in a stern tone, "You didn't do drugs, did you?"

I whispered under my breath, hoping my dad didn't hear her question. "No, Mom!"

I had to face it. Regardless of what happened that night, I was responsible. This was all my fault, and that was the hardest reality.

I'm the one who decided to go out for dinner and drinks. I chose to go to a party where I didn't know a lot of people. I could have just gone home after dinner, but I didn't. I had so much guilt and shame weighing on my chest. I even felt nauseated.

I had to find the strength to pull it together. I was scheduled to leave for Carson, California, the next morning for a weeklong work trip as a media team lead for the CrossFit Games. It was a big job—and an important one to me. I had dozens of volunteers, photographers, writers, and broadcasters relying on me to show up and deliver my best event-management skills.

I headed back home so I could pack for the trip. While it did cross my mind maybe I shouldn't go on this work trip, I kept telling myself Stella was safe. This was still a job I had committed to, and I was still under contract. As terrible as it sounds, I didn't want to let my work team down, too. I had already let my daughter down, pissed off my husband, and disappointed my parents. *Maybe the time away would be good for me. Maybe I would come home and things would be better.*

I pulled my hot pink suitcase out of my bedroom closet and flung it on the bed to start packing. My eyes were bloodshot, and my eyelids were pink and puffy from crying. It had been a rough day.

Jesse stormed into our bedroom and pointed to my suitcase on the bed. "You're really going to leave after what you did to Stella?"

I threw my arms into the air. "What do you mean? What am I supposed to do? This is my job. This has been planned for months. They are expecting me there. I am under contract."

Jesse grabbed the door handle as he walked out of the bedroom. He looked back at me. "What kind of mother leaves her child after this? I can't believe you!" He slammed the bedroom door shut.

All I could do was take a deep breath and release. I didn't know what else to say or do. I was emotionally drained at this point. I plopped myself onto the bed and fell backward. A part of me was still thinking some space apart would smooth things over for me and Jesse. I wanted everything to be good again. I tend to respond to trauma the same way, by continuously moving forward and going about life, telling myself "I am strong" and "I can get through this." I didn't feel strong, though, I felt ashamed. I felt unworthy of being a mother. Yes,

Stella was unharmed, and I was grateful to God for that, but Jesse and I were not in a good place and he had every right to be angry with me.

CHAPTER 3

FLYING INTO CHAOS

———

The next week in California was absolute torture. I had feelings of hating myself for leaving and just wishing I could take it all back. Jesse was barely answering any of my texts or calls—not even just so I could say hi to Stella. I knew something was up. I could feel it. When he finally let me talk to her, I had a huge sense of relief. She was so happy and cheerful. I missed her squeaky little voice so much.

Stella: "Hi, Mommy!"

Leia: "Hi, baby! I miss you. What are you doing?"

Stella: "I'm going to a consultation."

Leia: "A what?"

My heart sank. *A consultation? How does a four-year-old know what a consultation is?*

Leia: "Stella, let me talk to Daddy now. I love you, baby."

Stella: "I love you, Mommy."

Leia: "Hello? Jesse, you there?"

The call ended. He'd hung up on me.

My thoughts were running all over the place. *What was he up to? Why wouldn't he talk to me?*

I couldn't wait to get back home to figure out what was going on. I was extremely apprehensive. I knew something wasn't right.

In the meantime, I had to keep working. I had to keep pushing through and leading the media team as if nothing had happened 1,500 miles away back home. I was overseeing integral operations for media at the CrossFit Games, an event that draws fifty thousand spectators to watch more than five hundred athletes compete. It was my second year in this highly coveted leadership role. I wanted to perform well and meet the expectations of our event directors, but I was dying inside. I kept thinking I should have just stayed home. I couldn't stop thinking about Stella and wondering about Jesse and why he wouldn't talk to me. That was the story of my life: I was successful in my professional life, but I was struggling in my personal life.

I could hardly sleep the night before it was time to head back to Omaha. I arrived at LAX and sat in the terminal near my gate. Jesse still wasn't answering my calls. I just wanted Stella to know I was on my way home, but he wouldn't respond to my texts.

If you've ever had that gut feeling, your intuition telling you something is going on and it's not good, you know how loud it can be. I felt butterflies in my tummy, and not the good ones. I was ready to be home with Stella. I couldn't stop thinking about her little voice saying she was going to a "consultation." I kept wondering, *What kind of consultation?*

My cellphone started buzzing. It was my mom calling.
Leia: "Hello!"
Mom: "Hi, are you on your way home?"
Leia: "Yes, I am boarding soon. I'm at the airport."

Mom: "There's a sticker for you on the front door of your house from the Douglas County Sheriff's Office. You are being served for something."
Leia: "What?"
My mom's words hit hard. *Was Jesse going to a consultation with an attorney? Was he taking me to court? Was he pressing charges against me for what had happened? Was I going to jail for child neglect?* My mind immediately started thinking the worst.

My heart started racing, and I felt like I couldn't sit still. I grabbed my backpack with my laptop inside and walked over to the middle of the airline terminal to plug in my laptop. I flipped it open and immediately started pulling up the Nebraska Justice website to search public court records, which I had access to as a journalist. I couldn't type fast enough. I wanted to know what was going on.

First, I typed in my name. Then, I entered "2015" in the year field to narrow the search. I hit "Submit Search" and waited. Of course, the free Wi-Fi in LAX was slow to connect at the worst time. After about twenty seconds, which felt like forever, I saw it: Both our names, in Plaintiff vs. Defendant form and the words, *"Dissolution of Marriage."*

Jesse had filed for divorce just three days prior, the same time he was ignoring my calls and texts while I worked my ass off in California. I was furious. He didn't even give me a chance. No wonder why he was avoiding me and not allowing me to talk to Stella.

When I clicked on the files to open them, I was beside myself. I read through the court file thoroughly in disbelief. I knew how to decipher court files because that's what I did for years as a journalist.

I opened a supporting affidavit to find Jesse was also asking for temporary full custody of Stella. *He didn't even want me to have rights as a mother? What in the world was happening?*

The court affidavit read, *"The Plaintiff fears that, unless restrained by this Court, the Defendant may endanger the minor child, disturb the peace of the plaintiff and/or the parties' minor child, and may sell, transfer, assign, hypothecate, encumber, damage, destroy or otherwise dispose of the parties' property."*

I started trembling as I continued reading, *"The Defendant is a severe alcoholic and has been so all of her adult life. The parties attended marriage counseling within the past two years, and the Defendant admitted her alcohol abuse and the severity of the alcohol abuse, discussed the matter, but the Defendant refused to seek treatment or cease her abuse of alcohol. The Defendant is intoxicated two to three times per week and drinks to the point where she passes out or blacks out about once each week."*

Now I was pissed. He was completely exaggerating the truth and failing to mention he and I drank alcohol *together* most of the time. It didn't matter, though. I had no ground to stand on. His affidavit went on to detail the terrible night that will forever be impossible for me to forget:

"The Defendant endangered the minor child by an alcoholic episode on July 18, 2015. The Defendant drank at a bar throughout the evening, drove drunk to a relative's home where the minor child was spending the night, picked up the minor child from the relative's home shortly after midnight on July 18, 2015, without telling the Plaintiff, and drove to the family residence where the Plaintiff was asleep. The Defendant then left the minor child in her car seat, inside the Defendant's automobile in front of the family home and went into the house and

passed out in the living room of the home. The Plaintiff awoke Saturday morning, July 18, 2015, and at about 8:30 a.m., he discovered the Defendant passed out in the living room and woke her up. In questioning the Defendant, and contacting the home of the relative, Plaintiff realized that the minor child had been taken from the relative's home by the Defendant during the night. The Plaintiff then determined that the minor child was in the Defendant's car in front of the family home. The minor child had urinated and was soaked in sweat and crying. The car windows were closed and the doors were locked. Plaintiff took the minor child and cared for her throughout the day. The Defendant left on the following morning, Sunday, July 19, 2015, to spend a week in Southern California in connection with her hobby/part-time job with CrossFit. The Defendant will return to Omaha on Monday, July 27, 2015."

The court documents went on to say: "*The Defendant sent a series of text messages to the Plaintiff on Saturday, July 18, 2015, expressing her remorse at leaving the child in the automobile overnight, explaining that she only had five beers, but failed to acknowledge or express any concern for her alcoholism and the resulting actions and behaviors. Defendant attempted to explain the events by blaming others and hypothesizing that she may have been drugged at the bar.*"

If I have ever been kicked while I was down, this was that moment. I couldn't believe the man I thought had my back and loved me through sickness and in health, through good times and in bad, would completely blindside me like this. I felt so betrayed. I was so hurt. He was using this terrible incident against me to try to take my daughter from me. To top it off, he wouldn't even talk to me about it. I wasn't at a bar and my job with CrossFit wasn't just a hobby. I was angry, upset, and emotionally distraught.

I was living a nightmare and bawling my eyes out in the middle of the LAX terminal as I stared at my laptop, scrolling through the court file.

I shot off a text to him: *"You filed for divorce?"* I couldn't wait for a response so I called him immediately after. I was a bit shocked he actually answered the phone this time.

Jesse: "What do you want?"

Leia: "You filed for divorce? Really?"

Jesse: "Yes. You are a drunk, and I am done with you."

Leia: "So you're just throwing away our marriage and taking my child away from me? What is wrong with you? You didn't even want to help me. You just wanted to hurt me. You never even cared if I was drugged or if something happened to me."

People were already staring at me because I was crying and yelling into my cellphone, and all eyes were on me.

Jesse: "We are done! Stella is safe with me." He hung up.

I couldn't help myself. The emotions and the rage and the fear of losing my daughter took over. I let out the loudest shrieking noise I have ever made in the middle of one of the busiest airports in America—Los Angeles International Airport. People were all around me, but I didn't care. My life was crashing down.

Everyone looked in my direction. The passengers for my flight were lining up to board, so it was also time for me to go. As I was packing my laptop in my backpack, I noticed a security guard walking straight toward me.

The guard stopped in front of me and asked, "Are you all right, ma'am? We had some reports of a disturbance in this gate area." He stared intently at me.

I held back a sob. "I am sorry, sir." Tears were streaming down my face. "I have some personal problems, and I apologize. I am emotional. I'm sorry."

"You're shaking, ma'am. Can I get you a bottle of water or something?" He reached out a hand to me, but didn't touch me.

"No, thanks. I'll be okay." I pulled out the last tissue I had in my travel pack and wiped my eyes.

The security guard looked at me kindly and with empathy. "With all due respect, ma'am, whatever is happening in your life right now, I promise you it will get better."

"I hope you're right." My head dropped to my chest, and I covered my face with my hands.

He then asked, "You think you can keep it together for your flight?"

I looked at him and nodded my head up and down. I didn't really know if I could keep it together, but I had to try.

I grabbed my backpack and headed toward the gate. All of a sudden, I was no longer eager to go home. I was dreading it. I felt like such a failure. All sorts of emotions were running through my mind. I put on my sunglasses, as if they would keep people from seeing me. I just wanted to hide. I didn't want to make any more of a scene in front of the flight attendants or other passengers. I just wanted the chaos to disappear.

I boarded the plane, sat in my seat, and leaned my head against the window. As the plane took off, I said a prayer to myself. *Lord God, please give me the strength to get through this. Please don't let me lose my baby. In Jesus' name. Amen.*

The plane took off and ascended smoothly into the blue sky, but all I could feel was my life spiraling out of control.

CHAPTER 4

RELUCTANT TO REMINISCE

I thought I would sleep on the plane ride back home, but my mind was racing. I knew the woman sitting next to me could sense something was wrong because even with my sunglasses on, she could see I was wiping away my tears. I could feel her staring at me out of the corner of my eye, and I had a feeling she was the talkative type.

"Do you need a tissue?" she finally asked softly, pulling an unopened pack of travel tissues from her purse. "You can have the whole pack. I have extras."

I looked at her and smiled. "Thank you so much." I grabbed the tissues from her, and she continued to chat. "Do you want to talk about it?" she asked sincerely.

I took a second to think about it. I could already feel the shame and embarrassment creeping in. *What are people going to think of me when I tell them I am getting a divorce? Should I really tell this complete stranger what's going on in my life?* I knew she was just being friendly, but maybe venting and talking about it would actually help me. I took a deep breath, pushed my sunglasses to the top of my head, and turned toward her. "Well, I'm a little embarrassed to talk about this so soon, but I just found out my husband filed for divorce while I've been out of town for work."

Her eyes opened wide, and she just kept staring at me, waiting for me to continue the story. So, I did. "He won't even talk to me about it. I feel like such a failure. He filed for temporary custody of my daughter, too. He said I was a danger to my child. I don't know how I'm going to get through this."

As my tears started to fall, she put her hand on my shoulder. "Oh, sweetheart. Divorce is tough. I've been there, too. I know this may be hard for you to see and understand right now, but oftentimes a divorce can be a blessing in disguise."

Jesse and I had a lot of marital problems, but I never thought it would come to this point. I never thought there would actually be a time where we couldn't work through it. I never expected him to give up on us. I wasn't ready.

I continued to wipe my tears with a tissue as she continued, "I do know from experience you will become so much stronger and wiser from this. I don't know if you're religious, but I believe God has a plan for all of us. He has a reason for our struggles. You have to believe that."

I nodded my head up and down in agreement. "I do believe that, but right now this is just so hard for me to process. I can't imagine my life without my daughter. She's only four and she's my everything."

She looked at me intently and said, "You will get through this. I promise you."

I took another deep breath and leaned my head against the window, looking out into the vast blue sky. Her words were calming and exactly what I needed. Watching the plane climb higher and higher through the clouds was normally soothing, but I had so much worry in my heart. I feared the unknown, and I was angry with myself. *Why did I have to mess up? Why did I have to go out that night and ruin everything?* As the plane passed through blankets of clouds, I couldn't help but reminisce about happier times with Jesse. Despite our problems, I still loved him. I just didn't understand how he could want to throw away everything we built together, let alone take my daughter away from me.

Could I really lose custody of my baby girl? I would never intentionally hurt my child. Will anyone believe me?

The thoughts of losing Stella took me back to June 27, 2011, the day she was born and the happiest day of my life. I was induced around six in the morning. I remember being so excited to find out whether we were having a boy or girl. Jesse and I wanted to be surprised, so we didn't find out the gender beforehand. In my heart, I knew it was a girl. I was so excited to meet her and hold her. Her room was all ready to go. The turquoise walls were covered with colorful starfish, octopuses, fish, and turtles. We decided on an ocean theme since it was neutral for either a boy or girl. We even hired a muralist to paint it. Although Jesse already had one son whom I had been helping to raise for about four years, this would be my first child, and I was so giddy.

The doctor said she could feel the baby's head, and it was almost time to start pushing. I immediately asked, "Does the baby have a lot of hair?"

My doctor said, "I didn't feel any."

It sounds ridiculous to be worried about the baby's hair, but it's a Baez family trademark. All of the babies in the Baez family are born with full heads of hair, mostly dark, thick, and curly. My brother kept teasing me that my baby would be bald, and that's all I could think about. It makes me laugh whenever I think about it. As soon as the doctor pulled the baby out, I turned to Jesse and said, "What is it? What is it?"

He was in awe and couldn't get the words out. All he could do was stutter.

Finally, my doctor said, "It's a girl!"

My Estella came roaring into the world at 3:06 p.m., healthy as can be *and* with a full head of dark brown hair.

My doctor looked at me and said, "She has so much hair it must have been slicked back and I couldn't feel it."

We all laughed.

Still reminiscing, my mind traveled to a sunny, spring day in 2009 when Jesse and I were married at Our Lady of Guadalupe Church in South Omaha. We had a traditional Mexican wedding, incorporating the lasso, or "el lazo," a long rosary placed around us as a symbol of our unity. We also included the blessing of the thirteen gold coins, or "las arras," which the groom gives to the bride to symbolize prosperity and financial trust. These were important traditions in our culture, and we were excited to include them.

We had mariachis for the dinner and hired a live band for the dance. The decorations at the reception hall were immaculate and elegant, and it couldn't have been any more perfect. We were all about having a great time and wanted our guests to dance the night away.

No one would have guessed that just days before our wedding, both Jesse and I questioned whether getting married was even a good idea. We had gotten into a big blowout over money and had another fight the night of our rehearsal dinner about going out to the bar with our wedding party. Our relationship was up and down *all the time*. Our fights even got physical at times. I tended to be mouthy and sarcastic, which was worse when I was drinking. Jesse had a short fuse. That combination made our relationship tumultuous. Anything I did that he didn't like would set him off. I felt like I was walking on eggshells at times because I never knew what kind of mood he would be in. I still loved him, though, and he was a hard worker and loving father. He took me out on dates and opened my car door for me anytime we were together. He was the first man I ever dated to open my door for me.

Thinking about the good and bad times had my emotions all over the place. One moment I was smiling, and the next I was crying. Luckily, I had the pack of tissues from the woman sitting next to me. I still couldn't comprehend how Jesse could want to end our relationship. I also didn't understand divorce because my parents were married in 1982 and were still happily married. No one in my family was divorced, except (sometime soon) me. I felt so broken. I didn't want this life, and it was definitely not the one I had envisioned.

I started to worry. *What's my family going to think? What are my friends going to say?* For some reason, I started to think of my grandmother, Mary, my mother's mom. I remember her being so happy for me when I got married. When Jesse and I bought our first house together, she was overjoyed. Family and marriage are both huge parts of our Mexican culture, and my grandmother was so proud of me for getting married in the Catholic Church.

I looked up to her. She's the reason my mother is such an amazing, hardworking, compassionate, and loving woman with a tenacious spirit.

I know both my mother and I got our strong work ethic from my grandma Mary. I still remember the days—back in the late '80s—when I would ride along with my mom to pick up my grandma from her job at a meatpacking plant in South Omaha.

I was an extremely inquisitive seven year old. I wondered why my grandma came to the car all bundled up—wearing a winter jacket, a knit hat, and gloves—when it was so warm outside.

She told many stories about her job on the production line in a freezer-like area of the plant where she packaged meat and built boxes. She worked there from 1975–1994. She worked ten hours a day, six days a week, with very few complaints.

It stung my heart just thinking about how I would tell my grandmother I was getting a divorce. I didn't want to let her down. I didn't want to disappoint anyone, but this was my reality.

The irony of this whole situation was I could have avoided it if I could have just said no to booze that night. I even remember having a gut feeling to stay home, but I was persistent about getting away for a few hours. No matter what, it seemed like alcohol was always finding a way to bring problems into my life. I knew I didn't like who I was when I had too much drink, and I was aware of the issues alcohol caused in my life, but I was embarrassed to admit them. *Everyone else around me drank—my friends and my family—so why couldn't I?*

About five months earlier in January of 2015, I decided I was ready for a break from alcohol. Another sober attempt, but this time I really wanted to change. I wanted to be strong. I wrote about my sobriety aspirations in my journal.

JANUARY 1, 2015

One year without beer. Sounds easy enough, right? Well, probably not for me. I'm a beer girl. I love having a drink after work, indulging in a six pack on the weekend, maybe even more. My issue isn't alcoholism, at least I don't think. My problem is I'm social and have a lot of friends and family, and most of our gatherings happen where beer and cocktails are involved. That leads me to my next problem. I typically eat healthy all week, but when the weekend arrives, I drink and get hungover and eat bad, greasy, unhealthy food, packing on extra pounds. It's a domino effect that leads me back to square one. It's a vicious cycle. I've come to realize that I will never get anywhere in my fitness journey with alcohol or beer as a part of the equation. This year, I didn't want to make a New Year's resolution because I didn't want to break it. This year, I'm choosing to live healthier by going a year without beer. I am excited for this journey. Wish me luck!

JANUARY 5, 2015
When you decide to live without something, whether it's chocolate, cookies, or beer, you end up seeing it everywhere. I saw awesome beer sales, signs for cocktail hours, and happy hour specials. Booze just kept popping up. It was unavoidable. Normally, I would grab drinks with coworkers after my part-time job as a bartender, but I didn't tonight. Instead, I told them that I'm choosing not to drink because I want to live healthier. I believe that's a step in the right direction because I need them for accountability. I'm not gonna lie, I couldn't stop thinking about having a drink tonight. But I was strong. I have decided my health and being a great role model for Stella are my top priorities.

JANUARY 10, 2015
It's funny that I left off writing in my journal about being a good role model for my daughter and today my

three-year-old said, "Mommy, you've got a big belly."
She lifted up my shirt and said "Mommy, it's jiggly!"
Then I sat there and questioned what sort of example
I was setting for my toddler. Maybe this was a sign.
Her message hit me hard. This is enough reason to say
goodbye to the booze. It's time to lose the extra pounds.
I am tired of having a beer belly.

JANUARY 19, 2015
I'm still sober. Yes, I am proud of myself. This is actually
quite an accomplishment for me. I've managed to go
to my cousin's wedding, have fun, socialize, and even
dance without needing or relying on a beer to have fun.
In fact, I love that I don't feel like alcohol is controlling
me any longer. Rewind a few months, and I couldn't
have a few beers without wanting more. Rewind a few
more years, and there were times I've passed out drunk
on the floor. And no, it wasn't when I was a twenty-
one-year-old college girl. I was a working professional,
an athlete, and most importantly, I was a mother. But
I was a mess. I was sloppy and irresponsible. I'm so
ready for change.

FEBRUARY 10, 2015
I have an overwhelming sense of clarity. I feel like I am
closer to my goals more than I ever have been. Living
sober isn't about anyone except for me. Sure, it will positively impact my family. I'll be more attentive to my
daughter, I won't pick fights with my husband, and I'll
be happier and more pleasant to be around. But I'm
doing this to prove to myself that I can do it, and that's
not easy to explain to my drinking buddies and friends

and family who love the crazy, loud, drunk me. I've told a lot of my close friends and family why I decided to do it. Most of them understood, but there are a few who ask "why" and tell me, "just a few drinks won't hurt." But what most people don't understand is I am not wired that way. Rarely can I have just a few drinks. I typically drink to get drunk. So until I can learn moderation, I am saying no. It surprised me to learn that mostly everyone wanted to know my reasoning for not drinking. They assumed I was pregnant. So lately I have been telling people I am on a cleanse to be healthier. Most seem okay with that response and say "good for you," even though that's not the entire story. I know I don't have to explain myself to others, but drinking is so normalized in society that you become the oddball if you aren't drinking. I'm okay being different, I guess. I'll just continue to pray that I can stay strong. So, cheers to this cleanse.

MARCH 20, 2015
My marriage is even benefiting from my sobriety. Well, it's not perfect, but we have less issues to fight about. One of our consistent arguments has always been over alcohol. If we were both drinking, we would for sure argue and fight even more. Clearly, I'm much happier without alcohol. I feel so hopeful.

That was the last journal entry I had during that attempt to stay sober just months before the terrible night I left Stella in the car. I stayed sober for about four months. I couldn't handle the social life without alcohol, and I gave in.

My reality was I couldn't just have one drink. It was always one more. Keep the party going. I broke the alcohol fast at a friend's party and ended up getting so wasted I had to get walked into my house by another friend who I ended up yelling at because I was drunk. He was doing me a favor, and I was belligerent. I couldn't even walk, and he was being helpful, yet I was a jerk to him. I hated myself after those shameful moments, but I couldn't stop drinking.

As the plane landed in Omaha, I looked to the woman sitting next to me. "Thank you again for your kind words. They really helped."

She smiled at me. "Stay strong, and remember, no matter what happens, there's always a reason to be grateful."

She was right. Even though I was heading into a legal war with my husband and felt like my whole world was crashing down, I still had many reasons to be grateful. At the top of that list was my Stella. She was healthy and in great spirits, and I was ready to battle for her.

CHAPTER 5

LOSING MY EVERYTHING

———

I was back in Omaha, but it felt nothing like "Home, sweet home." My life was in complete disarray, and the first order of business was to go pick up my divorce papers from the Douglas County Sheriff's Office and officially be "served."

I felt like I was living in a Lifetime movie. *Is this really my life right now?*

I picked up the manila envelope filled with court documents at the Sheriff's Office and waited to open it until I got back inside my car. I stared at the envelope for a few minutes, hesitant to actually see what was inside. Finally, I opened it up.

Anxiety bubbled in my throat. I couldn't believe what I was reading.

I care more about social media than my daughter? I don't parent my child because I'd rather play sports or go out with friends? That's what Jesse and his supporters who wrote affidavits were alleging in the court documents.

What a bunch of bullshit. How could he make up lies, exaggerate the truth, and present them to the court as facts? Little did I know, that's what a lot of nasty divorces look like—a he-said/she-said drawn-out battle over who is the better parent. What a mess! I never expected to be in this situation. *How am I going to respond to these allegations against me?* I felt crushed. I didn't understand how the person who was supposed to stand by me through all of life—through thick and thin—could turn on me and depict me as a horrible mother.

I kept reading through the court documents and flipped to the next page, where I landed on a supporting "exhibit."

It was a picture of me passed out drunk on the kitchen floor of my home. It wasn't even recent. It was at least a few years old, but the image he wanted to paint was one perfectly depicted in that picture. It honestly didn't surprise me too much that he had saved that picture in his cellphone for years. Maybe he was keeping it as ammunition against me. Our relationship was unhealthy. We didn't support each other. We'd rather be at odds with each other—fighting, verbally abusing each other and cussing at one another. That was our normal, and it was soul-crushing.

The picture of me passed out and curled up on the kitchen floor was now a court exhibit. I had no way to deny that photo. I was exposed, embarrassed, and defeated. Even though the photo was old, it still showed me exactly the way he wanted the court to know me, and I had no one to blame but myself.

To top it all off, I still had to go home and live in the same house with him after being served. He still refused to talk to me. He slept downstairs in the basement and wanted nothing to do with me. It was like I didn't even know him. So cold, so distant. So unreal.

I had a temporary custody hearing scheduled for August 12, 2015, which was only a few weeks away, so I was scrambling to find an attorney to represent me. I Googled "Omaha attorney who will fight for mothers" and "Omaha custody attorney for women" and started calling each and every listing that popped up. It was a nightmare. The first few were unavailable. Jesse was asking the court for full temporary custody of Stella, and I had to fight it. He couldn't take my baby from me.

I left voicemails and filled out attorney consultation forms online. Finally, I decided to tap into my own network. I knew a lot of defense attorneys through my work as a journalist, so I started reaching out for referrals. I got several names of the "best of the best" custody attorneys, and they were all top-dollar, costing over $300 to $350 an hour. *Holy shit! Where was I going to get the money to pay for this?*

I didn't care. My daughter meant the world to me, and I figured I could take out loans or sell some personal property or do whatever necessary to pay for an attorney to help me fight for her. Of course, my parents offered to help me, too. I'll never forget my mother's words the day I broke down to her and told her how much my attorney would cost. "Don't worry about the money, Mija! We will figure it out. We will do whatever it takes for our Stella Bella!" My mother's words could always comfort me in times of chaos. It's not like my parents were made of money or anything, but they were hard workers. Even more importantly, they were my backbone and would do anything for my brother and me.

I reached out to one of the attorneys recommended to me. One of my friends called her "a bulldog in the courtroom." That's exactly what I wanted, an attorney who would fight tooth and nail for me. I set up a consultation with her in person and divulged all the details about the night I left Stella in the car and my tumultuous relationship with Jesse. I am not going to lie, her demeanor and her style of questioning were extremely intense and intimidating. I felt like I was on trial just sitting in her office.

"You are going to need to give me more details about that night if you expect me to defend you," she told me with a stern, straight face. "Who were you with? What kind of beer did you drink? How many miles was the party from your cousin's house?"

Her delivery took me aback a bit, and it took me a few seconds to respond. "I was out with my friend Daniel at a friend's going-away party. I drank Blue Moon beer in a bottle. I'm not sure of the exact mileage, but it's about a fifteen-minute drive. I can get you the exact miles, though."

She was tough, but *good,* and I was excited to hire her. About twenty minutes after leaving her office for our consultation, I received a phone call that because of a conflict of interest, she couldn't take my case. Apparently, her law firm partner had worked with Jesse in the past on a separate matter.

I closed my eyes, took a deep breath, and asked, "So what am I supposed to do? I literally have my court hearing in a few weeks, and I don't have an attorney."

Her tone was firm but sympathetic, "I'm sorry. You'll have to keep looking."

"Do you have any recommendations?"

She named a few people, but I had already crossed them off my list because they were unavailable days ago.

I waited to hang up my cellphone before I started screaming at the top of my lungs, *"Fuck!"*

Why wouldn't anyone help me? Was the whole world against me? It sure felt like that.

I went back to the drawing board. I had only one name left on the list of attorneys referred to me. I made the call, and by the grace of God, I was able to get a meeting scheduled.

I was down to the wire and frantic as hell. I just wanted someone to hear me out, someone to understand me and get to know who I really was. I was not the mother or woman being portrayed in these court affidavits. I was more than just that night—the terrible freak accident. *How could I be judged—all thirty-three years of my life—in one night? Would anyone believe me?*

At the first meeting at the law office, I found out I was actually going to be represented by a much younger, novice attorney of the firm for the initial temporary custody hearing. That made me so nervous. I wanted the veteran, not the rookie. I wanted someone with decades of experience who knew what they were doing, but I was desperate for anyone to represent me.

I was tired of having to tell all these attorneys about the night I left Stella in the car. I already felt like a piece of shit. I was full of shame, and it just brought up a flood of emotions every time I had to play that night over in my head.

After telling the young attorney about the incident, he looked at me and said, "Wow! You are in a bad situation! This is extremely serious!"

My jaw dropped. I felt like looking at him and screaming, "Duh! You don't think I already know this?" I was aggravated. *Was this attorney even on my side?* I just wanted to hear some positive feedback or hope in his voice, but there was none.

Finally, I got a tiny piece of good news a few days later: The judge granted me a continuance, giving me more time to prepare for the temporary custody hearing.

That meant I had a little bit more time to round up some character witnesses from my network of supporters who could submit affidavits to the court on my behalf and help show the true me: a loving, caring mother who would do anything for her daughter. I would also need affidavits from my friends about *that night.*

Would it be enough? This divorce and custody fight was set to be an all-out war, and my husband had taken the first shots. I had to fight back.

* *

The day I had been dreading, August 26, 2015, was finally here. I arrived at the Douglas County Courthouse early that morning with my father. I could always rely on my family to have my back, especially during such difficult times, but this situation was nothing like I had ever experienced. This was far worse and crippling to my mind. I couldn't even fathom what would happen if I lost my rights as a mother.

My father and I sat on a bench outside of the courtroom. I watched my attorney as he walked over to us. He told me only the attorneys would be going into the judge's chambers to discuss temporary custody, and I would wait outside.

I was hoping and praying the affidavits from my family, coworkers, and friends were enough to show my true character. I couldn't sit still, and the suspense of it all was killing me as we waited for my attorney to exit the judge's chambers.

About twenty minutes later, I saw the door start to open, and my attorney walked out. I was staring him down to try to read his expression. He walked toward me but wouldn't even look at me. I could feel in my gut this wasn't going to go well. I started to have a mini panic attack, thinking the worst of the worst.

Slowly, my attorney started to speak. "Well, you lost...," but before he could even go on, I abruptly interrupted him. "What? I lost? What does that even mean?"

My dad intervened to try and calm me down. "Let him finish, Mija."

My heart was pounding. I felt nauseated.

My lawyer started shuffling through his papers. "You lost temporary custody of your daughter. This is only temporary. Your husband will get full custody of Stella throughout the duration of your case or until you two can come to an agreement before that."

My entire body went numb. "Are you serious? Did you even stick up for me in there?" I yelled at him.

My attorney fired back quickly, "You have to understand this was a very serious incident."

I covered my face in my hands, "You don't think I know that? This is not who I am! Damnit, this is not the person I am. Something happened to me."

I tried to control the tears from falling, but it was impossible. I was crushed. *How could Jesse want to take my baby from me? Why couldn't we just settle our divorce amicably?*

I went from being with my daughter nearly every single day of her life to seeing her only twice a week and every other weekend. My whole world was flipped upside down. I was far from a bad mother, but this judge's decision had me questioning my own worth. I was losing my mind.

I was thrust into my lowest point mentally and emotionally, and I felt like my life was over.

CHAPTER 6

MY CHILDHOOD BEDROOM

———

Not only did my new life mean learning to live without my daughter, but I also had to find a new place to live.

As part of the temporary court order, Jesse also requested sole possession of the home we bought together in 2007, meaning I had to move out. I honestly didn't even want to fight with him about it. I wanted to be somewhere I felt support and love, and that wasn't in that home.

Especially in the days following the temporary custody hearing, Jesse was so cold to me. It was like he didn't even know me or hadn't spent nearly ten years building a life with me. I would just sit in our home and cry. He made me feel like I didn't even belong there. I would have left sooner, but I wanted to be with Stella as much as possible before this new reality set in.

Jesse was adamant about divorce, and as much as I begged him to listen to me, to hear me out, to understand my side, to give me another chance, there was no getting through to him. That was typical of his personality, though. He was all or nothing. He refused to compromise, and he was done with me.

Among all of the legal negotiations that happen in a divorce, I also agreed to let Jesse keep the house. The only downfall was I had no savings of my own to get a new place. I didn't even have enough savings for a deposit for an apartment. Divorce is expensive, my attorney fees were outrageous, and I was broke. I had to get on my feet financially, so that meant moving back into my parents' house, the home I grew up in on Missouri Avenue. I didn't even have to ask my parents to return home. They knew the pain I was in, and they wanted me there. It was as if they knew I needed to be at my home base, surrounded by support and love.

I was lucky to have a home to go back to and to have a supportive family who would take me in, no questions asked. I realize not everyone has a family to fall back on when life gets tough. I'm so grateful and thankful for my parents, but I would be lying if I said moving back home was picture perfect. It messed with me mentally.

As much as I wanted to go back home to be with the two most supportive people in my life, moving my belongings packed into totes into the home where I grew up felt like a demotion in life. I felt like I was moving backward. I had gone from being a successful professional, a journalist, a homeowner, a wife, and a mother back to square one. It was an awful reminder of how badly I messed up. Everything was just so heavy for me. I felt I was losing everything, all of it was ripped away, and it was all my fault.

To top it all off, I had to sleep in my childhood bedroom—the one still decorated like I had it in middle school, with teal-colored walls and glow-in-the-dark stars stuck to the ceiling. Gone was my own home and my big-girl room with big-girl belongings and décor I bought with my big-girl money.

It's incredible how quickly life can change. It's even more bizarre how the feeling of the unknown and uncertainty can overwhelm you as if you're drowning.

Some nights, I would just lie in my childhood bedroom and cry for hours. Losing temporary custody of my daughter made me ashamed of myself. I couldn't eat. I couldn't sleep. That was my new norm.

I, of course, couldn't help but think the worst. *What if I don't get to see my daughter again? What if my only child doesn't get to grow up with a mother? What had I done?*

Most nights, I would cry myself to sleep, my eyes so heavy and puffy from all the tears I could barely keep them open. I'll never forget one night in particular. Something was different about my room that night. The glow-in-the-dark stars on my ceiling stood out for some reason. They seemed so much brighter than any other night. I might have been a bit delusional from all of the emotions, but I could swear those stars were twinkling at me. They seemed to be staring back at me like they were trying to tell me something.

A weird sense of calm came over me, and in that moment, I traveled in my mind back to 1996 when I was eleven years old. I loved going shopping with my mom because it almost always meant she would buy me something, a toy of some sort, clothes, or candy. That day, it was glow-in-the-dark stars to decorate my room. I had seen those stars in the teen magazines I loved to read, and I wanted my room to look cool. As soon as we got home from Kmart, my mom helped me stick the stars on the ceiling. One by one, we put a small ball of putty on one side and stuck them up. I held the chair as my mom stood on it, reaching toward the ceiling. She hung some as did I; we did it together.

I was so excited that night—the first night sleeping underneath those stars. I was eager to see if they really worked. *Would they glow all night?* They certainly did. Before I fell asleep, I wished on each and every one of those stars. I was just a happy-go-lucky sixth grader with big dreams. I pointed at each and every star and shouted my dreams into the universe. "I'm going to be a professional ice skater." "I am going to make the volleyball team." "I am going to graduate college." "I am going to help the poor." "I am going to write a book." "I am going to get married." "I am going to be a mom." "I am going to live on the beach." I am sure there were a lot more, but those are the dreams I remember. I always had big aspirations, and I never doubted myself as a youngster. In fact, I felt safe when I was dreaming about the future and envisioning the possibilities.

Fast forward over twenty years, and that's exactly what those stars wanted me to remember. They were telling me to pick myself up out of my sorrow. They were twinkling at me to remind me that despite my divorce, losing custody of my daughter, and my demons holding me back, I could still go after my dreams. It was such an unreal moment. It was a spiritual awakening if you will. I had not prayed harder to God at any other time in my life. I believe God was using the stars as a sign to trust Him. I literally had this wave of emotion come over me.

All of these positive thoughts started streaming into my head. *I can still be great. Sure, I didn't want to be divorced. My parents had been married for more than thirty years, and I never knew anything about divorce before, but I could still be great. This wasn't the life I had envisioned, but my dreams are still out there. I can do this. I can freaking do this. This divorce doesn't define me.* Then, from that day on, I decided I was going to stay focused on bettering myself and keeping a positive mindset.

Those stars were the proof I needed to keep going. Those stars were my dreams, and they were still up on the ceiling glowing every night, even after all these years.

I never would have guessed small pieces of plastic could be so extraordinary, so pivotal, so life changing. That's exactly what those little glow-in-the dark stars on the ceiling of my childhood bedroom turned into, though.

I fell asleep with a new sense of hope and a new sense of purpose. I wasn't just going to let this divorce wreck my spirit or steal my drive. I was born to shine.

CHAPTER 7

FOUNDATION OF FAITH

———

Have you ever felt like you were seeing so many signs around you that you just couldn't ignore them?

The very next morning after that pivotal night with my glow-in-the-dark stars, I stopped to get a coffee at the gas station on my way into work. As I walked inside, a woman struggling to carry a large bag of ice to her car nearly tripped and fell. I caught her as I leaned against the door to prop it open for her.

As I helped her balance the bag, I asked, "Can I help you with that?"

The woman turned pleading eyes to me. "Oh, that would be great. Thank you. I have a bad knee."

I threw the bag of ice over my shoulder and carried it to her car. As I put it in the back seat of her car, she started to thank me profusely.

I smiled at her. "It's no problem. You're welcome."

She eyed me. "You must work out. You made that look like it weighed nothing."

I had to laugh. "Yes, I like to lift weights."

"You're strong! Well, thanks again."

"You're welcome."

I couldn't help but notice the woman's baggy blue T-shirt. The verse on the T-shirt was from Jeremiah 29:11 and read, "For I know the plans I have for you, plans to give you hope and a future."

I pointed to her shirt. "I love that Bible verse."

She smiled and said, "It's one of my favorites, too. Have a great day!"

I smiled and walked back into the gas station to get my coffee. I couldn't help but think of all the signs around me. *The stars last night, a complete stranger telling me I'm strong today, and the Bible verse on her shirt!* I knew I was being guided, and I was trusting in God to get me through this terrible time in my life. Despite all the turmoil and tension I had with my ex and all the chaos of a divorce, I felt uplifted in that moment. I still had a glimpse of hope to keep pushing forward.

Faith has been a stronghold in my family my entire life. I was baptized at Our Lady of Guadalupe Catholic Church in 1983 as a baby, went to CCD or "catechism" classes from kindergarten until sixth grade, and I even attended Catholic school for junior high. My parents felt I needed a little redirection after running around with the wrong crowd.

Nonetheless, God has been in my life, guiding me and helping me see past my fears, for as long as I can remember. I thank my parents for giving our family a foundation of faith and a mindset that better days were always ahead.

It seemed like just about everything growing up revolved around our faith in God. When we lost or misplaced something, my mom would encourage my brother and me to pray to Saint Anthony, the patron saint known as the finder of lost things. Whenever someone was ill, my mother would light a candle at church and say a prayer for them. When things were going well, my mother insisted our guardian angels were looking after us and blessing our family. Whenever I was acting up—yes I was a bit of an ornery child—my mom made sure I knew who was watching. "God is going to punish you if you keep acting like that," she would tell me.

Leia Baez (top left) poses with her parents and her brother in March of 2020. Leia calls her family her "rock" and her source of unconditional love. Photo by Leia Baez.

We attended church regularly and were involved in fundraising efforts for our church for many years. I can't recall a time in my life when I didn't rely on my faith for something.

I'll never forget receiving the Holy Sacrament of Confirmation in the eighth grade. It was my turn to walk down the church aisle to meet the archbishop at the front altar for a special blessing. I started to cry, tears streaming down my face and my arms filling with goosebumps, and I had no idea why. After going back to sit in the pew with my family, I told my mother about being emotional, and she quickly responded, "That was the Holy Spirit in you." I didn't even respond because I believed her. I felt something special that day, and I knew my mother was probably right.

A lot of my mother's strong faith was passed down from her own mother, my grandma Mary. Every single time I would leave my Grandma Mary's house, she would bless me with the sign of the cross and say a prayer before I got in my car and drove away. Any time we would drive by a Catholic Church, we would bless ourselves with the sign of the cross. Those strong religious beliefs brought me comfort. I learned them from my mom, she learned them from her mom, and my daughter Stella now follows along, too.

It was that same foundation of faith that has carried me through the darkest times of my life. It helped through all the sleepless nights when I first moved back to my parents' home during my divorce. So many times, my mom would rub my back and tell me, "Everything is going to be okay. Just keep praying."

So that's what I had to do—pray and stay faithful. I would soak in the claw foot bathtub at my parents' home and just cry. I would stay in the tub for hours and just think about my life, how everything changed so quickly, how I felt like my life was over, how I felt unworthy. I would rely on my favorite Christian worship music to bring me joy. It was tough, but the For King & Country hit song "Shoulders" always had a way of lifting my spirits. Soaking, praying, and hoping for a new day—that's all I could do. I felt so bad for my father sometimes because he would hear me crying down the hallway and I know he was hurting to see me in so much pain. Some days were better than others, but God was always there. He has a special way of showing up when we need Him most, when our hearts are shattered and our souls are shaken.

Jesse and I were at odds and couldn't agree on anything. Everything about our divorce was an all-out tug-of-war. We had no chance of working things out or trying to compromise and be civil. We were at each other's throats, and it was mentally draining. I just wanted him to let up and stop trying to make me out to be a terrible person.

It was devastating to know people were talking about me, judging my situation, and calling me names. All I could do was pray. Sometimes, I would fall to my knees and sob. Not having any control in my daughter's life was killing me. I never needed God more than in 2015. There was no worse feeling than not knowing where my life was headed and whether I would ever get to *fully* be in my daughter's life again.

Lord God, you know my heart. You know who I am. Please help me, guide me, and show me the right way. I just want my baby back. I say this jokingly, but God was probably tired of hearing from me. I literally prayed to Him every day and night, asking for guidance.

I felt like the only place I could turn was to my faith and my family, who loved me unconditionally. I had already lost friends and people who were close to my ex. Even former neighbors were gossiping about my life, and all I wanted was peace. So, I prayed, and I started to feel closer to God than I ever had. I put all my trust in Him.

One of the best perks about moving back home was having my mother around constantly. She always had a way to comfort me with her words, and she did whatever she could to make me feel at home again, comfortable, and content. I am so grateful for our bond.

On the nights I couldn't sleep or couldn't stop crying, my mother would walk into my childhood bedroom and sit with me on the edge of the bed. She sometimes would say something and other times she would just rub my back and sit in silence. She just wanted to be there for me, and I love her for that. No matter what the situation looked like, my mother always knew how to find the bright side.

"God wanted you to grow, and so he had to shake things up a bit," she would tell me. "You have to believe everything is going to be all right. Everything happens for a reason."

I was sure hoping so, and I trusted her. I was ready to get my life back on track. I wanted my baby back. I wanted *me* back.

CHAPTER 8

EMPOWERED BY EDUCATION

———

Education and going to school have always been my jam. Even when I chose to run around with the wrong crowds in middle school or when I partied too much in high school, I somehow always managed to get on the honor roll and be recognized for my academic achievements.

"Hitting the books," as my father would say, had always been a top priority in my family.

My parents instilled that in my brother and me at a very young age, when we were just elementary students. While my father attended a post-secondary trade school to become a printer, neither he nor my mother had the opportunity to attend a university to pursue higher education. They were hard workers, both holding jobs while they were still in high school. My parents wanted better for my brother and me, so they always hammered the importance of education to us. They wanted to see us excel more than anything.

My dad would always tell us, "You can do anything you want in life when you do well in school," and my brother and

I believed him. Well, we didn't really have a choice but to believe him. We had another thing coming if we ever brought home a report card with a "C" or worse. He made sure his point got across by stating, "You are not "C" students!"

Even though my brother Victor is seven years older than me, we have always been close. When it came to school, I always wanted to do better than him. I would bring my report cards home from elementary school and would have mostly 1s and 2s (equivalent to As and Bs), and the first thing I would say to my dad is, "Did I do better than Victor when he was in my grade?"

My dad would always smile at me and say, "Yes, you did, Mija!" even though my brother was more of a straight-A student and had me beat.

It was a healthy competition, that's for sure.

My brother was a stellar student and always near the top of his class. I had an incredible in-house role model my entire life when it came to always giving 110 percent. My brother has been the best mentor I could ever ask for, and he has pushed me to always strive for more.

Because of the example my family set for me, I loved being in the classroom. I loved everything about education, so much so, I earned a full-ride academic scholarship to the University of Nebraska at Omaha as an undergraduate. I was a Buffett Scholar, a program created by Susan T. Buffett, the late wife of Warren Buffett, one of the wealthiest and most successful men in the world and an Omaha native who still lives here. The Susan T. Buffett Foundation has awarded scholarships to roughly ten thousand college students in Nebraska over the past fifty years, giving minority students the opportunity to pursue higher education regardless of their economic circumstances.

I still remember opening and reading the letter stating I had been selected for this prestigious scholarship program. I was overjoyed, not only because I was proud of my academic achievements in high school and the killer essay I wrote when I applied, but also because I was able to erase the financial burden for my parents.

I always felt empowered in the classroom because I knew it was a steppingstone to achieve whatever I wanted in life. Schoolwork came easy to me (except college algebra, which is an entirely different story), but I still loved to party. In fact, I was in college when my alcohol habits got worse. I was drinking just about every other day, sometimes daily. There was always a "College Night" or a "$1 Drink Ladies Night" and a group of friends ready to go out.

I was still passing my college classes and maintaining an editor job at the college newspaper called *The Gateway*. Yet, I was using alcohol to bury my sorrows of an abusive relationship with a disloyal, narcissistic boyfriend. Again, same story—I was excelling on the surface but hurting underneath.

A few months after moving back to my parents' home in the fall of 2018, I experienced a divine moment. I saw an ad on television for Bellevue University, and I just knew it was a sign from God that I needed to go back to college so I could focus on bettering myself. I knew a master's degree would lead to better career opportunities, and now that I was a single mother living on a newspaper journalist's salary (let me tell you, journalists don't get into the industry for the money), I knew the time was right to go after my goals. I always saw myself working in government communications or media relations, so a master's degree in public administration was appealing to me.

Now that I was living back with my parents and they were always so helpful with my daughter when I had my visitation time with her, I knew they would be more than willing to watch her so I could study. It was the perfect set-up. *Was it meant to be?* I truly believed so. I had wanted to go back to college for a master's degree for several years, but while I was married, it never seemed like the right time financially. My husband didn't like the idea of me racking up student loans and more debt for us as a couple. If I'm being completely honest, I felt like my husband just didn't want me to keep climbing the ladder. I sometimes felt my success made him feel inferior or insecure, but it didn't matter anymore. We were going through a divorce, and I could be who I dreamed of being—no permission needed.

Even though I felt emotionally drained most of the time, I knew focusing on something positive and something that would make me feel empowered was the only way to lift me up during that darkness. The same week I saw the TV ad for Bellevue University, I also started seeing Facebook ads promoting online degrees and being able to work-full time while getting a degree at Bellevue University. That wasn't just great marketing; those were signs for me, and they kept popping up.

My friends thought I was a little crazy. They would ask me, "How are you going to go to graduate school in the middle of your divorce? Shouldn't you be focused on taking care of yourself? Shouldn't you focus on healing from this and focus on your custody case instead of worrying about graduate school?" For me, getting back into the classroom—even if it was online—was exactly what I needed to do.

Yes, I needed to heal. Yes, I needed to move forward, but I also wanted to provide myself with an opportunity to feel stronger and be lifted up during a time when I felt weak and not good enough. I know my friends were just looking out for me and wishing the best for me, but I needed this opportunity *for me*.

Studying, researching, and writing would keep my mind busy and away from all of the negative energy and emotions I had been dealing with since Jesse filed for divorce. I was tired of feeling heartbroken. I was tired of not feeling like myself and thinking my life was over and I was a failure. I had to empower myself.

So, I decided amidst the darkest time of my life, during a divorce and custody battle, I would refocus all of my energy and pour it into my own self-development. I would lift my spirits by focusing on something that made me feel good about myself: education. I knew going back to school would make me feel strong, intelligent, independent, and hopeful for the future.

As I sat at my parents' dining room table, I logged into my laptop, went online, filled out the application for the masters of public administration program at Bellevue University, and clicked "Submit."

After all, getting multiple college degrees was something I had wished for on my glow-in-the-dark stars as a kid. When I received the confirmation email that my application had been received, I knew God was leading me, and I was exactly where I was supposed to be.

CHAPTER 9

PURPOSE IN PAIN

———

I was at work when I received the email that I was accepted into the MPA program at Bellevue University. My program was scheduled to start in May 2016 with an anticipated graduation date of January 2018. I was absolutely thrilled.

The past ten months had been rough. Even just waking up and showing up to work on time was difficult, but I was still going to work five days a week to work as deputy online editor at the *Omaha World-Herald*.

I was quickly learning how heartache can make you lose your mind. My emotions were a roller coaster, and some days were much worse than others. I would sit at my computer in the middle of a busy newsroom and out of nowhere my tears would just stream down my face.

Sometimes, it would be for absolutely no reason, and other times I would be easily triggered when I saw photos of families and happily married couples on social media. It was just a reminder I didn't have a family anymore. I was heartbroken.

It didn't help Jesse was still throwing jabs at me. He sent an email to the editor of our newspaper's parenting website that suggested we write a story about leaving children in hot cars. He didn't name me, but he knew I would read that email and wanted me to hurt and be reminded of how terribly I had failed. It felt like he wanted to ruin every aspect of my life. I was being shamed on social media and rumors were swirling among mutual friends.

Before my divorce, I would use my lunch break to exercise in our building's gym. During my divorce, it became my sanctuary to go talk or let out my tears in private. Sometimes, I would just sit down on the locker room bench and bury my face in my hands and cry. I had good intentions to use my lunch break to work out, but most of the time I couldn't pull myself together. My good friend and coworker, Maggie, would accompany me to the locker room often so I could vent. Divorce proceedings are downright devastating, and Maggie was always a great listener and knew the right things to say to calm me down.

I needed positive vibes, and I finally got some when my graduate classes started. Meeting with my professors and the other students in the program online was a breath of fresh air. I started to feel good again, and I had something to look forward to every night. Yes, I actually looked forward to all of the homework. Just being in the graduate program gave me a sense of purpose and made me feel like I had a promising future, despite everything that was going on in my life.

Don't get me wrong, it was a lot of work. I would go to work from 9:00 a.m. to 5:00 p.m. and then come home and study until midnight most days. Thankfully, on the days I had my daughter, my parents were home to help watch her. My parents were my backbone, and they've always been there for me.

While I was feeling great about the possibilities ahead and obtaining a master's degree, I found myself relying on alcohol to deal with the stress. Some nights, I would sit at the dining room table at my parents' house writing a paper and finishing assignments while downing an entire bottle of red wine. You would think the incident with my daughter would have spooked me away from booze altogether, but it didn't.

I believed I was drugged, so I didn't see alcohol as the problem. That sounds so selfish, I know, but it's true. I saw myself as a victim of someone else's wrongdoing, and if I was drinking at home in a safe place, I would be fine. I would still occasionally go out drinking with friends, too, but I was so focused on finishing my MPA that I was definitely going out less.

Graduate school was a lot to handle, but other things were on the up in my life. A few months into my MPA program, I decided to start looking for a place of my own. I had already been living at my parents' house for almost a year, and I was ready to move on. My divorce was not final yet, but our trial date was coming up fast, and I just wanted closure. I wanted a fresh start and to have a place of my own. I looked at apartments, houses for sale, and even condos. I was shocked at the prices for a two-bedroom apartment, so I didn't make any immediate decisions, but I was feeling excited for the future.

I had been praying about new beginnings and trusting in God that everything would work out. Living with a positive mindset had to be my priority. It was way too easy to go back to the darkness if I thought negatively or worried too much.

I started journaling like crazy at least three to four times a week to keep my mind focused on good things. I regularly wrote down what I was grateful for and followed the advice of life coaches and thought leaders on social media. I even downloaded daily motivational apps on my iPhone such as "I Am" for positive affirmations to say aloud, and I downloaded an app based off Rhonda Byrne's book *The Secret* because I wanted daily reminders I was in control of my thoughts and energy. I wanted to attract goodness into my life and her book, which is based on the belief of the law of attraction, says positive thoughts can change a person's life directly.

I wanted my life to change for the better, and it was starting to happen.

Just about a month after starting graduate school, I got the best news of my life. My attorney called me and said I wouldn't need to worry about the August 30, 2016, trial date for my divorce. Jesse was agreeing to settle out of court and not fight me for joint physical and legal custody of Stella. That meant I was getting my baby back. I broke down in happy tears on the phone. Nothing else mattered in that moment because I was regaining custody of my daughter and getting the second chance I had been hoping and praying for every single day for the past year.

Our attorneys had advised us that settling out of court would definitely cost less than a trial and, since there were no further alcohol-related incidents with Stella, a judge would likely grant fifty-fifty custody anyway. Ultimately, it came down to Jesse's decision, and I was so relieved.

So many positive things were happening for me. I felt like God was answering my prayers left and right, and it just kept happening.

Five months into my MPA program, a new spark of motivation came over me when I came across a job opening online for a public information officer for Douglas County, the largest county in Nebraska. This was exactly the kind of job that would be a perfect fit for a master's degree in public administration and would allow me to still utilize my journalism skills. This was exactly the kind of career I knew could put me in a better financial position to thrive as a single mother. It felt like another blessing, so I applied.

About six months into my MPA graduate school program, I landed my dream job with Douglas County, which came with a pay raise and excellent benefits. I was ecstatic. I felt like it was God telling me everything was going to be okay. That I would still be able to afford my daughter's school tuition, and I could still make ends meet as a single mom, something I had worried about for months.

Only a few days later, my mother said, "Come take a walk with me down the block. I want you to look at a cute brick house for sale."

I had always loved brick homes, but the idea of living a block away from my parents and my childhood home seemed a bit too much. "Mom, I am not going to live a block away from you," I told her, laughing.

She turned at her front door and raised an eyebrow at me. "Why not? Let's just go check it out. Think positive."

We called our family friend and real estate agent to meet us at the house to check it out. Even though it was outdated a bit cosmetically, it had everything I wanted: a fireplace, wood floors, open space in the living room and dining area, and a huge backyard.

It all happened so quickly! Jesse and I were settling our divorce and no longer fighting for custody of our daughter, and a few months later I had accepted my dream job. Then, a few days after that, I was signing paperwork to close on the purchase of my own home for Stella and me. Yes, it was just a block away from my childhood home. Stella was so excited to be able to have two bedrooms, one with mom and one with her dad, and she was even more excited we lived close enough to walk to her Lita's house. Instead of calling my mother Grandma, all of the grandkids call my mom Lita (pronounced Lee-tha and short for abuelita, which is "grandma" in Spanish). I was excited, too.

My journey was finally moving in the right direction, and I felt energized. I just knew having a positive outlook on life and the power of prayer were on my side. God was doing some major work in my life, and I was grateful for everything.

As I got closer to graduation, I started getting exciting emails about cap and gown ordering information and graduation ceremony information. Then, there was an email with a call for commencement speaker applications.

I had dabbled in public speaking in college and won a speech contest my freshman year, educating the audience on how to perform CPR. I used an Annie CPR training doll as a prop and ran into the classroom with the Annie doll on the ground. I pretended she was a real person and I was saving her by showing the class, step by step, how to perform CPR. My speech instructor said my performance was outstanding and said I had a natural stage presence. From that day on, I've had a knack for public speaking. Even though it's considered to be one of the top fears among Americans, public speaking is a joy for me. Don't get me wrong, I still get nervous before speaking, but it truly lights me up.

So, when I saw the email calling for commencement speakers, I felt compelled to give it a shot and applied. The first round consisted of twelve students.

All twelve had to share their commencement speeches with a preview committee of seven university staff members. Then, three finalists were selected to present their speeches at the all-faculty meeting a few weeks later, and I was one of them. I had to call a friend on the phone before walking into the building to present that day so she could calm my nerves.

I was excited, but also extremely nervous. I prayed before-hand and gave it to God. *Lord, I trust you! If this opportunity is meant for me, it will be!*

The finalists were kept outside of the room so we couldn't hear each other's speeches. Then, it was my turn. The room was packed. At least one hundred faculty members were there.

When I was writing my speech, I knew I had to be real and authentic. In my experience as a journalist, I knew sto-ries of real struggle and perseverance were the ones that resonated with people, and I wanted to be engaging. So, for the first time publicly, I opened up about my divorce and feeling like I had failed as a wife and a mother. I explained how getting my master's degree at Bellevue University was the hope I needed during one of the darkest times of my life.

When I finished speaking, I walked back outside the room. I waited with the other finalists for the faculty mem-bers to cast their votes for the speaker who would address the graduating class of 2018. Then, a staff member walked over to us and made the announcement. "Our commencement speaker will be...Leia Baez!"

Chills ran throughout my body and I was overwhelmed with excitement. I knew that moment was meant for me. I knew God had brought me there. It was the first time I felt my pain and my failures could bring good into my life. I was full of hope!

CHAPTER 10

POWER IN YOUR STORY

My glow-in-the-dark stars from my childhood bedroom had made such an impact on me that I knew I had to include their backstory in my commencement speech. I even decided to pass out glow-in-the-dark stars for all three hundred graduates on the day of commencement. I ordered two bulk bags of them on Amazon. During dress rehearsal the day before commencement, I set them out one by one on each of the chairs set up for graduates. It was a souvenir for all of their hard work and a reminder for them to remember their achievements, but also to "Dream Big, Fail Hard, and Never Give Up!" That was the title of my speech.

The morning of commencement was a bit of a rush. My nerves were going crazy, and I had to get up extra early, around 5:30 a.m., to get my makeup done. I had been practicing my speech for weeks, so I was ready.

When I arrived at the Mid-America Center in Council Bluffs, Iowa, across the Missouri River from Omaha, I had to go through a side door to get backstage. I felt like a VIP. I was escorted to my private dressing room. I really felt like a superstar. Behind the scenes, I took pictures with the chancellor of Bellevue University and recorded a few snaps on Snapchat. I took a few selfies with some other staff and another speaker, Ron Blumkin, a well-known local businessman, and was having so much fun talking to everyone. Everyone kept congratulating me and telling me what a huge honor it was to be the commencement speaker. I totally felt honored, but I was anxious to hit the stage.

I can still remember how clammy my hands felt. I was nervous sitting on that graduation stage, underneath the bright spotlights. That thick, polyester graduation gown was hot, but the bobby pins holding my graduation cap to my long curls were the real problem. They were digging into my scalp like daggers. I was afraid to even move my head a little and lose my cap.

At that moment, though, I was so grateful. I was happy to see so many relatives there to celebrate with me. I was proud to show my family I could overcome. I could persevere.

My nerves were jumping as it was my turn to approach the microphone and the podium—in front of hundreds of graduates and their families. My heart was racing, and I could feel the boob sweat. My hands wouldn't stop sweating. While I was extremely excited about being selected as the commencement speaker, I was also hesitant about sharing my story. Opening up and being vulnerable about raw details of my divorce and my feelings of shame, embarrassment, and failure was scary.

Sure, I was already a storyteller after having worked as a journalist for many years, but that was sharing other people's stories. This would be the first time I spoke my truth, publicly and on stage in front of strangers. My heart kept telling me I was right where I was supposed to be, that I needed to open up and share my story to give others hope. So, I trusted that feeling and I didn't look back.

I walked up to the podium with my speech notes in hand. I knew I would be too nervous to memorize the entire speech, so I had to have my notes as backup.

As I approached the podium and adjusted the microphone a bit, I heard a loud shout from the crowd echo throughout the arena, "Way to go, Leia!"

I smiled and got close to the microphone and told the crowd in a funny but embarrassed tone, "That's my dad!"

The audience erupted in laughter. As much as I wanted to feel embarrassed about my dad yelling at me, it made me proud to know he was proud of me. He also helped me to make the crowd laugh and lighten the mood, so it worked out perfectly.

I took a deep breath, made sure my notes were in order, and began the commencement speech that would forever change my life.

President Hawkins, Executive Committee, Board of Directors, faculty, graduating class of 2018, family, friends, and guests—welcome.

I am truly honored and humbled for this opportunity to represent the class of 2018 and share a piece of my journey with all of you today.

My name is Leia Baez, and I am an Omaha, Nebraska, native, growing up right across the river in South Omaha.

I want to start this story by taking you back to 1996. Now, I know that's a long time ago, so if you're having trouble going back that far, just think "Heeeeeyy Macarena!" That was the number one song on the charts at the time, and I can't tell you how many times I did the Macarena in my bedroom mirror. I was eleven years old and in the sixth grade and this glow-in-the-dark star was the coolest bedroom accessory around. (I held up one of the stars at that moment.)

Leia Baez delivers her commencement speech for Bellevue University on January 27, 2018. Court. Bellevue University Courtesy Photo.

That summer, my mom helped me decorate my entire bedroom ceiling with those stars, and I remember wishing on every single one of them: I'm going to make the volleyball team. I'm going to be a published writer. I'm going to graduate college. I'm going to get married and have kids. I am going to be a professional ice skater. Okay, so that last dream didn't actually come true, but I have been very fortunate to have accomplished many of my aspirations so far.

I did well in high school, earning a full-ride academically to the University of Nebraska at Omaha. I received my bachelor's degree in journalism and became an award-winning journalist for my hometown newspaper. I bought my own home, I got married, and I was blessed with the most beautiful baby girl, Estella.

I was achieving the dreams I had envisioned for myself one by one, but like many of you probably know, not everything goes the way we want it to. Challenges and obstacles can really throw our journeys off track!

I mean...let's face it. Hard times are inevitable, and at some point, every single one of us will have to deal with hardship.

Around this time two years ago, I was in the darkest place of my life. In just a matter of days, my whole world turned upside down. I was getting divorced and facing a custody battle and it took a toll on me. It was unlike anything I had ever experienced before. I was beside myself emotionally. I was heartbroken. I felt ashamed, embarrassed, and I believed that I had failed as a wife and a mother. I even lost friends, but worse... I lost touch with who I was as a person. This was not the life that I had envisioned.

During my divorce, I moved back into my parents' home so I could get on my feet financially. That meant moving back into my childhood bedroom—the same bedroom where I stuck all of those glow-in-the-dark stars on the ceiling, and they were still up there.

I remember crying in bed one night and looking up at the ceiling, wondering, Is this a demotion in life? Am I really sleeping in my childhood bedroom under those same stars when I'm in my thirties? How can I be failing when I've been so successful?

That next morning, something came over me. What I realized was that regardless of what I was going through in that moment, I could still accomplish my goals because my dreams were still out there. Those stars on my ceiling were the proof I needed to keep going. They were my dreams, and they were still up there, glowing every night. Now that may sound cheesy, but trust me, I would have never thought that this small piece of plastic could stand for so much and be the reminder I needed to keep chasing my dreams.

Later that week, I saw a commercial for Bellevue University on TV, and it hit me. That was the light I would need during the darkest time of my life.

Instead of focusing on the negative, I was determined to empower myself so I could be the best mother, best professional, and best leader possible.

That's exactly what Bellevue University has done for me.

Bellevue University was the hope I needed in a time when I felt unworthy. Amidst the hardest situation I have ever been through in my life, Bellevue proved to me that my story was far from over. Becoming a Bruin showed me that regardless of my setbacks, so many opportunities were still out there for me.

My professors became more like mentors, and my grad school colleagues who started as strangers became friends (Congratulations, TEAM MPA). The staff at Bellevue was with me every step of the way, even when they knew it would not be easy for me. My advisers made sure I had every resource to attain success, even encouraging me to apply for a scholarship that I later won. For my experience at Bellevue University, I will be forever grateful.

To the Class of 2018, you are talented, hardworking, and dedicated. We come from different backgrounds and hail from different states and countries across the globe. We are different in age and have different career goals. Yet we all still have one thing in common: We have dreams. I mean, come on... we didn't just do all of this work to wear these fancy gowns and rack up student loans. We are on a mission to better ourselves, to be successful and to make a difference. Today is a celebration of that.

Let's also celebrate the challenges that force us to grow. As I was putting my thoughts together and working on this speech, I couldn't help but get a little emotional. My struggles and dark times have made me so much stronger...fearless, even, and I am so proud of how much I've grown through this journey. When you choose to focus on the positives even during hard times, great things can happen. I have learned so much about myself, about overcoming adversity, and about always trusting God's plan.

I know that stars don't shine in the light, and neither do we. It is during the darkness that we are forced to grow and learn who we are. So, don't run away from those difficult times; embrace them.

Take risks and get out of your comfort zone. Believe me, I questioned giving this speech a hundred times, but I felt compelled to share my story in hopes of inspiring just one of you to never give up.

There will be people along your journey who want to dim your shine, but don't let them. Surround yourself with supportive people who want to see you rise to the top. If it weren't for my parents and my family who have always had my back and were so willing to help with my daughter so I could study, I wouldn't be up here today.

Promise yourself you'll never let giving up be an option. Whether it's losing a job, a bad relationship, or a failed project at work, I want you to know that your toughest battles will bring forth your biggest breakthroughs.

I want you to know that tough times don't last, tough people do.

Since beginning my master's program at Bellevue, not only did I land my dream job as a public information officer for Douglas County, Nebraska, but I finally moved out of my childhood bedroom underneath those stars and was able to purchase my own home.

My glow-in-the-dark stars came with me. I keep one of those stars at my desk at work and another in my weekly planner. They remind me of how far I've come and that no matter what life throws at me, positivity always wins.

Now, in traditional Oprah fashion, you get a star, you get a star, everybody gets a star. That's right! Class of 2018, take these stars as your reminder to dream big, fail hard, but never give up. Put this star in a place where you'll see it regularly and remember that you can overcome any obstacle when you choose to stay positive and believe in yourself.

Your success will be determined by how you handle the setbacks. The tough times help us grow as leaders.

No setback can actually set us back if we don't let it.

To the Class of 2018, to everyone here today, and to those of you watching online: Let's not be afraid to fail because failure often turns out to be the start of something so much greater. Congratulations, Class of 2018! Thank you!

The applause was so loud, and there were so many smiles in the crowd. My heart was full. As I exited the stage, I felt overwhelming relief for speaking my truth. Being authentic and vulnerable was scary, but it felt good—therapeutic, even. I remember thinking all I wanted was for my story to inspire one person. If my story could help just one person, then it would be worth it for me.

As I walked back to my assigned seat with my fellow graduates, a woman in a cap and gown grabbed my arm. She whispered to me, "Thank you so much for sharing your story. I am going through a custody fight with my son's father, and I didn't even want to come to graduation today, but I'm so glad I did. I needed to hear your story. Thank you! I promise you I will never give up!"

Wow! I had to hold back my emotions. My heart was overflowing with joy. That was a pivotal moment for me. All of the nerves and anxiety before my speech didn't even matter anymore. My story had helped one person, and that's all I wanted. Mission accomplished.

CHAPTER 11

A MESSAGE THAT MOVES

———

I was still riding the high from speaking at commencement that morning in January 2018.

Earlier that month, I was even featured in an online news article by Bellevue University highlighting my time in graduate school and the message I wanted my speech to bring to the audience.

"I hope my story inspires my fellow graduates to never give up—even during the most difficult times in life," I said in the article.

I had no idea just a few months later that speech would change my life forever—in the best way possible.

On May 3, 2018, I received an email from a media company called Goalcast. Here's what the email said:

Subject line: Leia—Inspire 10 million with Goalcast

Leia,

What would it mean to you if you could inspire millions of people with your powerful message?

You know the world needs inspirational messages like yours now more than ever. This is why we make authors, speakers and coaches with meaningful messages go viral online. With partners such as Tony Robbins, Brendon Burchard, and Lisa Nichols we are committed to making a positive impact in this world.

Leia, the message that you shared at Bellevue University is impactful and has the potential to go viral online. This is why I would like to give you the opportunity to be featured on Goalcast.

Here at Goalcast, we have over 10 million organic followers on Facebook, 8 million monthly site page views and a monthly page reach of 400 million. From helping authors sell their books to motivational speakers sell their online courses, we love aligning our marketing strategies with our partners to positively impact their business along with our viewers' lives.

Since videos are only rising in popularity, our production schedule is booked weeks in advance. I'd love to reserve a spot for your empowering message and to do so I need an open line of communication between our teams.

So, do you want to have a viral video with millions of views?

No way! *This can't be real,* I thought to myself. I was familiar with Goalcast and the inspirational videos they post on social media. I had seen their work before and loved it. *Could they really be interested in my story? How did they even find my speech?* I wanted to make sure this was a legit request, so I started researching the sender's name. I was blown away when I found he was a real person and an employee of Goalcast. I got goosebumps and responded to the email.

Mark,

This is absolutely a dream come true. I watch videos on Goalcast weekly, and I've been inspired by so many of them. I would love to share my message and do whatever I can to hopefully lift the spirits of others who may be down or going through a hard time.

I've been praying and hoping for an opportunity like this. Thank you, thank you!

Please let me know what the next steps are and how I can make this a seamless effort!

All my best,

Leia Baez

What a full-circle moment. I had watched some of these Goalcast inspirational videos during my most difficult times, including right after my first court hearing when I lost temporary custody of my daughter. Now it was my message Goalcast wanted to use to inspire others. Talk about mind-blowing! I was thrilled and kept the conversation going with the Goalcast employee. Turns out, his team found my video by "searching and curating" YouTube.

He said, "Your speech really resonated with our team members, which is why we decided to feature you and get in contact with you."

I was in awe.

First, I had to give them approval to edit my video and then approve the edited version—they cut it down from about fifteen minutes to three minutes—which took a little time.

Finally, on May 22, 2018, Goalcast posted my speech for millions of its followers on social media.

It didn't take long for my Facebook notifications to start blowing up. I had messages on Facebook and LinkedIn from women and men from all over the world thanking me for courageously sharing my story and giving them a sense of hope. They called my speech "incredibly powerful," "inspiring," and motivating." I was giving advice to people all over the world who were dealing with similar situations as I was. It was truly bizarre!

Dave in France was probably one of the hardest conversations for me to have. His business had failed, his wife had left him, and he felt like his life was no longer worth living. It was heartbreaking. I prayed for him the night he messaged me on Facebook, and I was grateful to hear from him a few days later. He said my speech resonated with him because he, too, had felt like a failure as a husband and father. He was also relying on his faith to keep his spirits up.

Alyzabeth in Texas was feeling overwhelmed with life when my speech came across her Facebook newsfeed. She messaged me on Facebook to tell me I had lifted her up when she needed it most. As a wife, a mother, and a full-time employee, Alyzabeth said she didn't know how she was going to make it through her college courses. She told me she wanted to be a great role model for her daughter, showing her it's never too late to chase your dreams. We became friends on Facebook and stayed connected.

She recently messaged me again to tell me she graduated magna cum laude with a bachelor's degree. "Your words came when I was tired of pushing," Alyzabeth wrote in a Facebook message. "I kept going."

Then there was Amelia from New York City. Our stories were extremely similar, and she said hearing my speech gave her goosebumps. "I just saw your speech on Goalcast and *wow*! You are a phenomenal speaker," she wrote. "I just wanted to say thank you for being brave and sharing your story. I'm going through a divorce, too, and I never expected my life to be like this. I'm going to watch your speech whenever I need a reminder there are better days ahead!"

Talking to so many people around the world who had similar struggles was helping me more than I expected. It showed me I wasn't alone. I wasn't the only person who had been through a rough divorce and custody battle. Yes, I know that should be obvious, but when you are deep in a situation like that, you feel so alone. I was surrounded by love from family and good friends, but I still felt alone at times.

Little did I know my speech eventually would reach more than 6.5 million people online. Even Jay Shetty, one of my favorite motivational speakers, shared my speech to his millions of followers on his Facebook page. Other motivational websites shared it, too.

My cellphone was buzzing nonstop with text messages and calls from my relatives who couldn't believe I had turned into a viral motivational speaker overnight. My cousins joked they wanted my autograph, and my friends couldn't believe it.

To know overcoming my hardships was inspiring to millions of people was surreal, but it was also the best feeling in the world. To know my pain had a purpose felt indescribable. I give all glory to God because I was truly led by my faith to go to graduate school, to apply for the commencement speaker opportunity, and to open up and share my darkest times. God guided me through it all.

The opportunities this one viral speech brought into my life were truly incredible. I was asked to be a speaker at several local events for a variety of audiences, including church groups, youth groups, and a women's leadership group.

I was blown away when I received a message the week after my speech posted on Goalcast from a media executive who was interested in sharing my story on her London-based radio program. Soon after our episode aired, she proceeded to tell me she also wanted to feature me in her faith-based magazine in London. She said she wanted me to be the cover story. *Me on the cover? Wait, what? Me, a cover girl?*

I was also invited to be a speaker at one of her women's leadership events in London. I ended up speaking virtually at the conference in April 2019. That officially became my first paid speaking gig, and I was elated.

Being recognized as an inspirational speaker internationally was by far one of the biggest honors after being featured on Goalcast. I again had to thank God for aligning me with all of these opportunities to share my story and bring hope to others.

I continue to share my story at events because I absolutely love helping people. The speaking engagement requests continued to roll in, and I couldn't believe I could actually make money by sharing my story. I was on cloud nine. This was my element, and I knew this was exactly what I needed to be doing.

Leia Baez was featured on the cover of the London-based magazine *DOZ* in November 2018 after her speech went viral and the magazine publisher heard her story. Photo by *DOZ*.

I was a featured guest on several different podcasts, I was interviewed for a variety of radio shows, and I loved every minute of it.

I was able to find my purpose in pain and truly live out my dream of being a motivational speaker, but none of this would have happened had I not gone through my darkest times. None of this would have happened had I not opened up to share my truth. My dark times helped me to discover my passion for motivational speaking.

I knew in my heart it was meant to be.

CHAPTER 12

MADE FOR MORE

—

While I was inspiring millions of people around the world with my story of overcoming, I felt a bit like a fraud.

I wasn't being completely transparent about my struggles. In other words, I didn't open up about *everything* I had been going through.

Just hours after I finished my commencement speech, I was finishing my sixth or seventh mimosa. I had met up with some friends for bottomless mimosas at a restaurant in downtown Omaha to celebrate my graduation. Once I start drinking alcohol, I tend to get a little carried away. Come on, "bottomless" means unlimited, and I wanted to get my money's worth, of course (insert eye roll at myself). The truth is, I never really had an off button when it came to booze. Once I started, it was hard to stop unless I was passed out or puking. That evening, my parents were also throwing me a graduation party at a neighborhood bar and restaurant. I already had hours of day drinking under my belt before I arrived. I danced and drank through the night, taking shots of liquor with Red Bull to stay energized. That hangover lasted a few days, and I remember questioning why I was so inclined to drink all day. *Why couldn't I say no?* I was a binge drinker, and I didn't know how to stop.

That same story for me continued: I was successful on the surface, but underneath I was struggling. Things were going well for me professionally, but I still knew in my heart I needed to stop drinking. It was holding me back, and I always had terrible anxiety and a hangover from Hell after a night of partying. I kept wondering why I continued to do this to myself. In a society where alcohol is everywhere and binge drinking is normalized, I had no idea how to say no. It was a cycle I didn't know how to break. I felt trapped, and in my heart I kept hearing a voice say to me, "You are made for so much more."

I needed to talk to someone about it. I wanted real advice from someone other than friends and family, and my therapist seemed like the best place to start. So, I booked an appointment.

About a week later, I walked into my therapist's office and plopped down in his chair. I had made a fool of myself on a recent night out at the bar, drinking too much and acting belligerent in front of some of my former coworkers, and I was extremely embarrassed. I didn't even remember what had happened until my friend texted me the next day. Ugh, I was a mess!

Dr. Jeffrey Stormberg, a psychotherapist in Omaha, had been familiar with my issues since 2013 when I first started seeing him. He knew about my alcohol dependency problems and all the good and bad in my life. After the incident with Stella in 2015, Dr. Stormberg and I both agreed it would be best if I cut out alcohol entirely, and I did for a while. I never drank around Stella, but as soon as she would go with her dad, I drank. I eventually just lied to my therapist every time I would see him and told him I was drinking in moderation, when in reality, my alcohol use had actually increased.

I considered it my coping mechanism and my stress reliever, even though it actually was the opposite for me.

Why was this so hard for me? From the time I was thirteen and took my first sip of a beer in middle school, alcohol has always been a huge problem.

It didn't matter what I was doing, I felt like everything I did revolved around alcohol. Dinner with friends, networking events, vacations, football tailgates—I always had a drink in my hand. I didn't drink every single day, but when I did drink, it was a domino effect of negative behaviors in my life that would last for several days. Drinking would turn into a hangover and eating bad food, skipping the gym because I was tired, a bad mood, and just not feeling my best.

Even with all of the happy hours that turned into after hours, I still wasn't happy.

In conversation with my therapist, I started to think about all of the times alcohol had a negative impact in my life.

In 2005, I had several fights with my best friend from California to the point she didn't even want to be my friend anymore. She stopped talking to me for several months after a trip to Las Vegas went sour because I was disrespectful to her while intoxicated. Luckily, she forgave me and is still one of my best friends and greatest mentors.

At an NFL football game in Kansas City in 2010, I somehow ended up in the middle of a fight among tailgaters, got pushed around, and then tripped and went head-first into the curb, chipping my front two teeth. Had I not been drinking, I would have had better coordination and balance and could have kept myself from falling. Jesse and I had a fight and I was upset, so I drank way more than I should have. It didn't matter if I was upset, angry, happy, or celebrating, I always had an excuse to keep drinking. Not even the $4,000 I had to pay for new porcelain veneers could keep me from drinking.

In June 2013, I got so intoxicated at my cousin's bachelorette party one of my aunts had to hold me up on the dance floor. I actually didn't even remember dancing. I was nicknamed "Bernie" after that night as a joke because my cousins said I was flapping my arms around and dancing with my eyes closed like "Bernie" from the 1989 comedy *Weekend at Bernie's*. It makes me laugh hysterically now, but I was so embarrassed at the time.

I've hurt a lot of people, too, saying rude or obnoxious things when I was drunk. To say I can be a mean drunk is an understatement. I wasn't always rude or mean, but I had no control over my response to alcohol and how I would act.

These are just the situations I can actually remember. Geez, I can't even begin to think what other terrible or hurtful things I have done in twenty-three years of drinking that I don't know about.

During some of the hardest times of my life—a divorce, a custody battle, an overflow of self-doubt—my relationship with alcohol only got worse. I relied on alcohol to reduce my stress when it actually increased my anxiety. It became a crutch for me, and I was easily triggered when I would argue with Jesse or disagree with him on anything related to co-parenting Stella.

Like everything else, I had prayed and prayed for guidance. *How can I possibly live a happier life without alcohol when it's all around me? Please help me, Lord. Guide me, Jesus! I don't want to be an alcoholic anymore.*

Then in the fall of 2019, my life took a very emotional turn. I had a health scare after my gynecologist found a tumor the size of a small cantaloupe in my uterus on September 11, 2019.

It would require emergency surgery, and the best option was a partial hysterectomy to remove my uterus and the tumor together. I was devastated. The idea of no longer being able to have children weighed heavily on me. I envisioned I would someday get remarried and have more children. Clearly, I hadn't yet learned I was not in control in this life. It was a hard decision for me, so I got a second opinion from another doctor. His opinion was similar. The fibroid was large, and the safest way to remove it would be to have a hysterectomy. I was concerned about being healthy for Stella. I wanted to be sure this fibroid was benign and didn't show any cancer cells.

The difficult news kept coming. In October of 2019, my uncle who had been like a father figure to me my entire life died. He was only fifty-nine. His death sparked something in me that's often hard for me to explain. It pushed me to reflect a lot. It made me think about my values and how I was spending my time. I started thinking, *I'm in my thirties—what if I only have twenty more years to live? How do I want to spend my time? What do I want my life to look like? Am I on track to accomplish my goals? Am I on the right path to success?*

To put it simply, the answer was no.

I knew I needed a change. I knew I was wasting a lot of time boozing, and that wasn't aligned with who I wanted to be. I knew it was time to quit. I was ready to be done with anything that wasn't going to bring joy to my life or move my needle forward when it came to my goals. I started researching time-management programs and the best goal-setting methods. I hired a life coach, and I was ready to fully commit to being intentional with my time and energy.

On November 6, 2019, I celebrated my dad's birthday with my last beer. I was scheduled for my hysterectomy in a few days, and they recommended no alcohol for at least three to four days prior to surgery to keep my blood from getting too thin.

On November 11, 2019, I had surgery to remove the tumor and my uterus. All I can remember is sitting down on the cold operating table, preparing to get the anesthesia, and I was out. The next thing I remember is waking up in the operating room and crying hysterically. My nurse who was wheeling me around in the bed kept asking if I was all right. I felt emotional because I had a dream of my uncle who had passed away the month before. It was so real and crystal clear, and I'll never forget it. I saw him standing in a white circular light and I could hear his loud, boisterous laugh. He grabbed me by the shoulder and looked me in the eyes and said, "You don't have to drink!" in an assertive, yet sarcastic way. It was like he was saying, "Duh! You can choose not to drink!" That's when it hit me. I told myself, "I *don't* have to drink. I *can* be different. I *don't* have to do what everyone else is doing."

It was an "Aha!" moment for me.

I decided at that moment, still in the hospital, I would never drink again. I was doing it for me and for my uncle. Also, I wanted to break the generational curse of alcoholism on both sides of my family. I wanted to show the younger generation of my family what's possible. I wanted Stella to know she can accomplish anything her little heart desires. I wanted her to see there's more to weekends than boozing and hangovers. I didn't want her to think the only thing to do when she turns twenty-one is to rent a party bus and get drunk like I did. I wanted Stella to see we can overcome our biggest setbacks and accomplish our dreams. If trauma can be passed down through generations, then so can healing. I knew I had to lead by example.

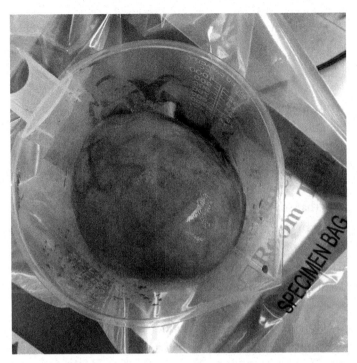

A cantaloupe-sized tumor that weighed about 2.5 pounds was removed along with Leia's uterus in November 2019. Pictured above is the uterus with the tumor inside. Photo by Dr. Jill McTaggart.

I knew God had brought me all of these experiences in my life intentionally. I knew there was no coincidence. God had a plan for me, and I believed the dream about my uncle was a part of that. Real transformation requires real honesty, and I was ready for a new life. First, I had to get real with myself. I was tired of my own shit. I was over the fact that I couldn't be my best self because alcohol was holding me back.

It didn't help to know some of my friends didn't want to see me change. Some even said, "Awww, I'm going to miss drunk Leia!" Others would tell me, "You're not an alcoholic. Just have a few," but I was an alcoholic. Just because I was successful in my career didn't mean I wasn't struggling in my personal life. I've come to realize some people have this odd perception a person who struggles with addiction must be homeless and without a job, but that's not reality. The truth is we all struggle. We all have down times, but it's the rebound that matters. I was ready for my big play.

I am not afraid to admit I was a huge party animal. My family even joked my theme song was Eddie Murphy's 1985 song "Party All the Time" because that's what I did. (I still love that song, as cheesy as it is.) I was so ready for the real party in my life to start, the one where I show up 110 percent for myself, always giving my best. I wanted the party where I prioritize my health, both physically and mentally. Most importantly, I wanted the party where I get to be fully present for Stella.

I knew I had my work cut out for me because I had tried quitting before, but this time felt different. I had the support of my own guardian angel, my uncle, and he believed in me.

CHAPTER 13

SOBER IS SEXY

———

I knew getting sober meant I had to become so comfortable with myself there would be no need to cope with alcohol to turn off my emotions or numb the pain. The new life I wanted so badly—peace, self-love, being a strong role model for my daughter—all required the hardest sacrifice from me. I had to let go of my old life—completely.

I used to think about alcohol a lot before sobriety—just about every day. *Should I have a drink after work? Where will I party this weekend? Who am I drinking with? Which happy hour is best? How much money do I have to party this week?*

Even when shopping for new going-out clothes, alcohol was on my mind. Most times, I would opt for buying jeans so I didn't have to worry about flashing anyone in a skirt or dress if I got too drunk. Those were my real thoughts.

Alcohol ruled my life. *Will this wedding have an open bar? Do we need to pregame before we go out?*

It wasn't until I began researching how to live alcohol-free that I learned I had actually been binge drinking for several years. Before a night out, my friends and I would almost always start with "pregaming" at one of our houses—a little drinking before we went drinking.

If it seems excessive, it was. Binge drinking, according to the Centers for Disease Control and Prevention (CDC), is defined as "four or more drinks in a single occasion for women and five or more for men." Heavy drinking is defined as "at least eight drinks per week for women and fifteen for men." I was a binge drinker and a heavy drinker most of the time.

Unfortunately, excessive drinking is actually not uncommon. Our society has normalized binge drinking, and it has become common in popular culture for moms to joke about downing an entire bottle of wine to make it through the day. You can't get on social media without seeing memes depicting exhausted women guzzling wine—also referred to as "mommy juice"—in giant glasses. "Wine o'clock" has become the time moms look forward to as a way to get through the stress of parenting.

According to the Nebraska Department of Health and Human Services, alcohol is the most commonly used substance in the state. The rates of binge drinking continue to be higher in Nebraska than the US.

In July 2021, researchers at carinsurance101.com used data from the CDC and the US Census Bureau to find the highest rate of binge drinking across the country. In its report, my hometown of Omaha ranks as number six on a list of "15 Large Cities with the Worst Drinking Problem." Their research also shows 21.7 percent of adult Nebraskans binge drink compared with the national rate of about 16 percent.

I was a part of those staggering statistics.

You would think there is nothing to do in Omaha except to drink, but that's not true. I was determined to find out what life was like on the other side. I knew if I was going to stay sober, I needed a complete change of scenery. No more bar hopping or happy hours, even if I could order a seltzer water or non-alcoholic beer. I needed to do a complete one-eighty on my life, starting with my environment. Everywhere I went and the people I surrounded myself with had to change. I had to remove myself from tempting situations.

I knew I would need serious accountability. I attended a few AA meetings back before I was divorced, but I wanted to try something different. I wanted to lean on someone whose story I was familiar with and who I knew personally. The very first person who came to mind was a woman named Joelle, whom I had met years ago at a CrossFit gym. I had seen her inspiring pictures and short stories on social media about her own triumphs since living alcohol-free, and her words always left me feeling motivated and encouraged. I reached out to her in a Facebook message, asking for advice on how to stay on track with this new lifestyle.

Joelle had already been sober for about three years at this point, and what she gave me completely changed my life. She invited me to dinner with her friend, Karyn, who had reached out to her on the same day I did, also asking for advice on living sober. I had never met Karyn before dinner, but we all instantly clicked as if we had been best friends for years. We talked for hours that evening, sharing similar stories of how alcohol held us back and turned us into women we weren't proud of. We vowed to keep each other accountable and support one another in our sober journeys. We even named ourselves the "Sober Support Sisters."

From that day forward, I no longer felt alone. I wasn't the only successful woman who struggled with alcohol. I wasn't the only strong woman who couldn't say no to booze or lost count of the blackouts. That dinner with my Sober Support Sisters changed my life for the better. I knew with my whole heart after that dinner I could stay sober. What once seemed like the most daunting challenge in the world now felt exciting and doable. Joelle shared incredible details of how her life improved dramatically, and I wanted that, too. I wanted to be so much healthier, save money, get out of debt, improve my fitness, and have the clarity to love life. Most importantly, I wanted to have the clarity to love myself. I had a new spark for sobriety, and I will forever be indebted to my great friend and mentor Joelle for her constant motivation and for proving sober is sexy. She's one hell of a Sober Support Sister.

Whenever anyone asks me how I stay sober, my number one answer is my faith and my belief God didn't just put me on this Earth to be ordinary. Coming in at a very close second is accountability and my incredible Sober Support Sisters. Having someone a phone call or text away is critical on the hard days—and there are plenty of them. This journey can be a roller coaster, and having someone in your corner who understands what it takes is priceless. Third, stay busy and fill up your schedule with activities and hobbies that bring you joy. I love how living sober reignites your passions because you have so much more time for the things you once put on the back burner for booze. I've been able to get back into weightlifting, yoga, meditation, mentoring, and coaching my daughter's volleyball team.

Living alcohol-free isn't just a test of my willpower and strength every single day, it's also a reminder I can overcome and do hard things.

On Christmas Day 2019, just about a month into my sobriety journey, I was ready to fall off the wagon. Holidays—especially when Stella was with her father—were triggers for me. I would get emotional and upset, missing my baby girl, and the first thoughts that would creep into my mind were about alcohol. I was literally ready to walk out the door and head to a neighborhood bar when a friend of mine showed up at my house with Heineken 0.0, the first non-alcoholic beer I had ever tried. It was so bizarre how simply sipping on a glass bottle could completely kill my craving for alcohol. I was fine after having just one non-alcoholic beer, and I remember thinking to myself, "I *can* do this!"

I had to switch my mindset to stay focused on my future. Who I had the potential to be had nothing to do with my mistakes of the past. The successful mother I wanted to be wasn't contingent on my failures or my traumas or anything I've been through. I could still be exactly who I dreamed of being. Day by day, I counted my victories and stayed committed to expressing how I felt in my journal.

The following journal entries always remind me of how far I've come.

JANUARY 16, 2020
I woke up in a cold sweat. Crying hysterically, I literally jumped out of bed. I couldn't believe I did this. I committed to living sober, and I failed. I let stress get the best of me, and after an argument with Jesse over text message, I caved. I drove to the store and picked up a twelve-pack of beer and came back home and drank every single one of them until I passed out. Why can't I stop drinking? Then, it hit me. I picked up my cellphone and looked through my text messages. I didn't see any texts with Jesse. I looked at my bank app on my phone, and I didn't have any charges at the store for beer. I let out the biggest joyous scream, "It was just a dream."

But it was more of a nightmare. I had heard about drunk dreams before from my Sober Sister Joelle and others in the sober community, but I never experienced one of my own until last night. Today, I am seventy days alcohol-free. I am so grateful to say I am still sober. That dream was extremely realistic and a reminder of the shame and guilt I felt whenever I drank. Sobriety really is a one-day-at-a-time journey. Every day I get better. Every day I get stronger.

I think we go through things in life to grow through them. I think having a benign tumor in my uterus and then losing my uncle were both signs from God. Was He asking me to think about my health and put my wellness first? I believe so. I knew it was time to take back control and live a life I could be proud of. The benefits I am already experiencing at seventy days sober are incredible. My energy levels are through the roof. I have clearer skin, I feel motivated, and I am sleeping better. I am in this badass mode, and I love it. We all get to a point where we are tired of our own shit, and that's exactly how I felt. I was ready for change, and I'm so glad I have.

MAY 7, 2020

Today was a good day. I don't know why I think of Ice Cube every time I write that, but no, really, today is amazing because I am celebrating six months alcohol-free! Woohoo! This is something I've never done in my adult life, except for when I was pregnant with my daughter. Even during my pregnancy, I would have a glass of wine every now and again. I'm a little overwhelmed with emotion because I've been drinking alcohol since I was thirteen years old—that's twenty-three years of putting booze into my body.

I have to sit in this moment and truly appreciate it. Today makes me reflect on all the time wasted, all the money wasted, and all the moments I regret. I know I shouldn't regret anything, but man...I was a terrible drunk. I was in my own way for a long time. I was overweight, I was mentally foggy, and I wasn't fueling my passions like I know I could. I knew that if I wanted to be my best, then I had to say goodbye to the booze. So this morning, I woke up and cried. I was so overjoyed and full of hope to have made it this far. Six months is a lifetime for someone who was drinking two to three times a week to the point of being drunk. I have to give all glory to God for giving me the strength and faith to push through the hardest moments and cravings. I wanted to give up so many times, but I kept pushing. Every time I would see a special discount on beer at the store or come across a happy hour event on social media, I would cringe a little. I would literally have a discussion with myself in my head before repeating, "No, I can do this. I don't need to have a drink. Alcohol is not a reward."

I would be lying if I said I wasn't a little sad every time this happened over the past six months. "Why can't I just have a few drinks like some people? Why can't I drink in moderation?" I am thankful for all of the people who pick me up when I have moments of doubt. Having accountability warriors or sobriety supporters is hands down the number one reason I am still sober today. I am, additionally, so grateful for my family and friends who are always there to remind me why I started this journey: to find the best version of me and to be the best I can be for Stella.

I couldn't have done this without my Lord and Savior, Jesus Christ. I also do it for my uncle who passed away in 2019 from cancer. I do it for a lot of people in my family who struggle with alcoholism and don't believe that there's a way to change or don't believe they have the power to fight through addiction. Well, I'm proof we hold that power.

NOVEMBER 7, 2020

Wow! I can't even believe I've made it here. Never in a million years did I ever think I could proudly say I am one year sober, but here I am, and I'm shouting it from the rooftops. I did it! Today, I am one year alcohol-free, and I feel unstoppable. I mean, staying sober for an entire year during a global pandemic is a miracle in itself. I knew I wanted to celebrate this important milestone in a unique way, so last week Stella and I drove a few hours from Omaha to Des Moines, Iowa, to meet up with a good friend of mine who works as a professional photographer. I thought a photo shoot for Stella and I would be an awesome keepsake for my sober birthday. I also wanted to take a fun celebration picture, so I decided to buy small balloons that spell out "One Year, No Beer" and use them in some of my photos. My photographer loved that idea.

It was just a quick getaway for a few days, but it was memorable. Driving back home from Des Moines provided me a lot of time to reflect. I felt like an entirely new person—far different from the young woman I used to be.

Leia Baez celebrated her one year of sobriety with a fun photoshoot in Des Moines, Iowa. Photo by Ginnie Coleman Photography.

I thought about the first time I smoked marijuana with some friends in eighth grade. I was drinking and wasn't in my right mind to say no. In high school, I had a similar story with some friends who offered me cocaine at a house party to sober up. From that point on, any time anyone at a party had cocaine, I was getting in line for a "bump." It was my drug of choice. It woke me up, and I enjoyed feeling energized. Would I have ever started using drugs if it weren't for my alcohol abuse? I honestly don't think so. I made a lot of terrible choices because I was drunk or constantly chasing a buzz. I was often careless and even reckless when I was drunk.

As I continued the drive home, the clouds in the sky had moved together and appeared to look like angel wings. I took that as a sign from God to give myself some grace. I may still be a work in progress, but I am on the right path. I felt it both then and now.

For me, the goal was never just sobriety; it was always and will always be about discovering my best self.

In the last year, I've given myself more time to work on my passions as a writer, motivational speaker, and mindset coach. Becoming a coach landed in my lap after I attended a leadership conference and a friend of a friend reached out to me, seeking assistance with a writing project. She knew my work and also heard me speak at an event. It was one of those things that felt meant to be. I love that when I'm not working my full-time job, I now have the time to help others live their best lives, too.

I love that my values and goals now align with how I spend my time. Instead of relying on alcohol to relieve my stress, I focus on exercising and spending time with family. I'm extremely grateful for all the bad times in my life because if I didn't have those struggles, I would not be where I am today. I have experienced so much growth in my life, and now I feel compelled to help others. I want others to know that regardless of our setbacks—fear, anxiety, drug and alcohol abuse, self-doubt, or feeling unworthy—they can overcome. If I, of all people, can live a happy, successful life without alcohol, so can anyone else. Now, I'm having more fun than I ever have because my healing journey is progressing and I'm finally starting to see who I am meant to be!

JUNE 20, 2021

The longer I'm sober, the more realizations I have. As of today, I have been alcohol-free for 591 days. I have openly shared my sobriety journey on social media and in the Omaha World-Herald newspaper as a community columnist. I was even a guest on a local news talk radio show to discuss living alcohol-free. I share my journey because I want to give others hope. I can't help but tear up as I write this because I still have so many friends and family members who struggle with addiction. I get messages weekly on Facebook from friends who are struggling with alcoholism and asking me for guidance and advice. The stress of the pandemic only made alcohol abuse worse for a lot of people. What I've realized is that no matter what our struggles are, we are never alone. I love that I can serve as a source of motivation and inspiration for people who are struggling.

I'll never forget the Facebook message I received a few day ago. Jack, a childhood friend with whom I attended elementary school and someone I hadn't spoken to in years, asked if I could give him a ride to detox. He said he was ready to finally quit drinking alcohol after struggling with addiction for years. I had to help him. If I didn't help him, I knew I would regret it. When I arrived at his apartment, he didn't answer his phone. I was able to sneak into his locked apartment building behind another resident. His apartment door was unlocked, and he was passed out drunk on the couch at 8:30 a.m. Several empty pints of vodka were scattered all across the floor of a filthy studio apartment. I felt like I had stepped into the scene of a movie. I woke him up and helped him to my car. He couldn't even walk because he was so intoxicated. When we arrived at the detox center, the nurses couldn't admit him because his blood alcohol level was above 0.40. I was advised to take him to the hospital instead. Jack said he hated the hospital and didn't want to go. This wasn't his first time at detox or the hospital to attempt to safely withdraw from alcohol. I didn't have a choice. So, I took him to the hospital anyway. Jack was admitted, but it wasn't long before he went into a rage, ripping the IVs out of his arms and attempting to walk out of the hospital. His mood had completely changed, and he said he no longer wanted my help. The hospital staff told me he had done this before—at least twice. I had spent my whole morning trying to help him, and the reality was I couldn't do anything for him. It didn't matter what I said to him or how emotional I got. The only way Jack could get help was if he was willing to help himself. I felt defeated, and my energy was wiped out. Yesterday, he messaged me drunk again. I encouraged him to go back to the hospital to get help, and he refused.

It was heartbreaking, but I've learned I am not going to be able to help everyone who reaches out to me, but I'll keep sharing my story and do the best I can to spread hope and show that living sober is possible.

CHAPTER 14

TRAUMA TO TRIUMPH

———

Sobriety didn't magically solve all of my problems or make my life easy, but it allowed me to uncover years of pain and embark on a much-needed healing journey.

The hardest work in life will always be the work we do to better ourselves—to heal, to learn who we are, and to love ourselves unconditionally.

I can't honestly remember the last time I truly loved myself. In addition to my alcoholism, I'd had body image issues since I was a preteen, and I was in unhealthy relationships most of my life that made me feel unworthy.

Fortunately, sobriety brought me clarity and love for myself again. It was empowering to be able to control my alcohol addiction because it allowed me to realize I could now accomplish anything I ever wanted. I felt unstoppable.

I still had a desire to understand who I was at my core. I wanted to pull back the layers and discover what was behind my addiction and so many poor decisions in my life.

After the divorce, I wanted to understand what was behind my cravings to drink, so I started to write down what I was feeling every time I had the urge. On top of the obvious reasons like stress and boredom, I quickly realized I drank as a way to escape from being alone in my own home. Every time I was alone was a reminder I was divorced and by myself. It was a cruel replay of my failures and a slap in the face that I was now a single, struggling mother. So, I drank. I was so accustomed to going for drinks or meeting up with friends every time Stella would go with her father that I never had a chance to be alone with my feelings to process my divorce or my past. I just kept pushing on like the strong, resilient woman I was raised to be. I was running away from my feelings to avoid some deep wounds. I quickly learned how I responded to trauma was by running away from challenging times and compartmentalizing my emotions.

Once I finally had the courage to stay home and sit with my feelings, I experienced a lot of tears and sleepless nights. I was full of so much worry and paranoia because I no longer had control over Stella's whereabouts or who she was with when she was on her father's parenting time. I couldn't help but think the worst.

Just a few months after starting my sober journey, I woke up in a cold sweat from a terrible nightmare. It was a flashback of my own childhood trauma when I was sexually molested when I was about five years old by a great-uncle I barely knew. He was visiting the home of my great-aunt who babysat me when he lured me to a spare bedroom. I can still see him raising his index finger and tapping it to his lips to remind me what he was doing was a secret. That disgusting pervert still haunts me.

Stella was about five years old, too, when my flashbacks were the worst. My mind must have been associating her age with my own trauma, and it was messing with my head big time. I couldn't sleep. I couldn't eat. I felt so messed up mentally. My stomach was in knots every time Stella had to leave me.

Then it hit me. That sexual abuse as a child was so scary and uncomfortable that I had compartmentalized it for decades—almost thirty years. I didn't tell my mother about it until I was thirteen. My abuser was already dead by then, so we never talked about it again. Throughout my teenage years and as an adult, I kept pushing down flashbacks of the abuse, but it got to be too much for my sober brain. I was in my mid-thirties when I first shared the sexual abuse with Dr. Stormberg, my therapist.

I burst into tears and could hardly speak. I had let that trauma linger inside of me for so long.

Dr. Stormberg talked me through my feelings around the abuse, and I had so many questions. Why did that pedophile have to violate me? Was this the reason I was a rebellious teen? Was this why I started drinking alcohol as a teenager? Was this why I was drawn to unhealthy and abusive relationships with men?

Dr. Stormberg helped me to understand the trauma I had experienced wasn't my fault, and it was okay to let go of the shame and guilt around it. Dr. Stormberg told me trauma and substance-abuse issues often go hand in hand, with many people learning to deal with trauma by self-medicating with drugs or alcohol. While I would never truly know how much of a negative impact my childhood trauma had on my life, I had proof it was causing harm to my mental health. The flashbacks and my paranoia surrounding my daughter's safety were signs of post-traumatic stress disorder.

Between my therapy sessions with Dr. Stormberg and countless hours of researching childhood trauma, I felt like I was finally able to connect the dots and better understand how my own experiences in life had impacted my behaviors and decisions. I felt like I was getting to know myself more and more every day.

Dr. Stormberg has been a blessing in my life and helped me to see that even though healing is hard work, it's worth it. Simply talking about the abuse and understanding how trauma can linger with people if we don't do the work to heal was eye-opening. It was freeing to be able to finally talk about something I was so ashamed to discuss for so long.

As I started to dive deeper into decoding myself, I actually looked forward to staying home by myself. I would cozy up on the couch in my favorite pajama pants and fuzzy socks to read and research. I read a ton of "quit lit," which is what the sober community calls books about sobriety, and also a ton of online articles on healing from trauma. As I mentioned earlier in the book, educating myself has always been my go-to empowerment tool. I have always felt like I was giving back to myself and taking myself to the next level when I commit to learning something new and gaining knowledge.

During my Google searches, I came across trauma research by Dr. Richard Tedeschi, a professor of psychology at the University of North Carolina at Charlotte and a licensed psychologist in practice for over thirty-five years.

Dr. Tedeschi coined the term "post-traumatic growth," or "PTG" in the early 1990s. The basic concept of PTG is positive personal transformation can occur in the aftermath of trauma. So in addition to PTSD, I could actually come through my trauma wiser, stronger, and more resilient.

I was intrigued. I read he had created a self-help workbook called *The Posttraumatic Growth Workbook*, to help people move toward personal change and development and take a stressful or traumatic situation and use it as a turning point for personal growth. It's a workbook that provides exercises to show readers how to strengthen themselves through the great pain of loss or trauma. I wanted to check it out for myself, so I ordered it on Amazon.

The Posttraumatic Growth Workbook helped me realize how much shame and guilt I carried with me because of my childhood trauma. That sexual abuse forced me to believe I was damaged and unlovable, which was far from the truth. The workbook helped me to see my symptoms related to trauma and realize I was not alone. In fact, experts estimate about three-fourths of adults over sixty-five have been exposed to at least one traumatic event during their lifetime, and depending on the definition of traumatic event, the figure may be even higher.

After I started to reflect and complete some of the work, I realized I had experienced several traumas in my life I could list in the workbook's exercises: sexually molested as a child, physically abused by a longtime boyfriend in college, drugged and leaving my daughter in the car overnight, getting divorced, losing custody of my daughter, and fighting a custody battle in court.

While I did experience PTSD from my childhood trauma because I was coping with alcohol and drugs and having flashbacks and nightmares, I also experienced PTG. The traumatic situation with my daughter, my divorce, and losing custody of my daughter turned into years of positive personal growth, a deeper sense of spirituality, higher education, career advancement, and most importantly, sobriety.

Dr. Tedeschi pointed out PTG is possible for anyone. He said you can take any traumatic situation and learn and grow from it so you can be the best version of yourself.

I loved learning there was hope after trauma. I could actually benefit and grow from the traumatic experiences I've gone through. I was so interested in the concept of PTG that I reached out to Dr. Tedeschi to share my story with him and ask him some questions.

Dr. Tedeschi described trauma to me as "anything that makes life feel uncontrollable or unstable. Traumatic events challenge our ability to make sense of what's going on."

Then he solidified what I believed to be true: "It's very common that trauma and substance abuse are linked."

The beautiful part about my journey and why I'm inclined to share this story is because I want people to know it's never too late to heal. It's never too late to revisit the deep wounds you are running from and feel better about your life. You can find peace. You can move on. You can let go. It took me a long time to get here, but I am on the right path.

Dr. Tedeschi said even my decision to write this book and be so open about my life is a part of my healing journey. "Writing your book is an attempt to make a coherent story out of what happened in your life," he said. "It's easier to leave the past behind instead of letting it haunt you, and a memoir provides that opportunity. It's a way to make peace with the past."

During my research on childhood trauma, I also came across an incredible book by my idol Oprah Winfrey and Dr. Bruce D. Perry called *What Happened to You? Conversations on Trauma, Resilience, and Healing? Conversations on Trauma, Resilience, and Healing.* I found so many great quotes in this book, but my biggest takeaway was the negative impact you can have on your life when you don't do the work to heal from trauma.

"If you have experienced trauma, but haven't excavated it, the wounded parts of you will affect everything you manage to build," Oprah said. "We block our blessings because we don't feel we are enough."

Another powerful quote in that book came from spiritual teacher Gary Zukav, who said, "When you find an addiction, do not be ashamed. Be joyful. You have found something that you have come to Earth to heal. When you confront and heal an addiction, you are doing the deepest spiritual work that you can do on this Earth."

Uncovering who I am at my core has been the most challenging yet rewarding work I've ever done. I know it's critical for my growth, but it's also quite uplifting to know I can make sense of my mess and heal from my past.

My own behaviors started to make sense now.

After the terrible night I left Stella in the car, I went on with my life as usual and went out of town for work. That's what I knew. That was my trauma response. As much as it killed me inside that I left, I know now that's the behavior I have repeated my whole life—to run away from anything difficult and compartmentalize the emotions I don't know how to deal with.

After being sober for almost a year, I finally had the courage to talk to Stella about the night I left her in the car. I had never talked to her about it before, even though she has done her own therapy sessions after the incident and during the divorce. I first got the approval from Dr. Stormberg to talk to Stella about that night because I didn't want to cause her to have any harmful flashbacks.

When I asked Stella about that night, she said she remembered wanting to go inside the house, but she couldn't get the car seat unbuckled. "I just remember I wanted to go inside, but I couldn't get out," she told me.

I apologized profusely and told her it was a terrible accident.

She said, "I know you don't want to hurt me, Mom!"

Even six years later, the pain was still there for me, but talking about it with her definitely helped. It was part of my healing.

I believe having honest conversations with my daughter and learning tough lessons together will only make her better prepared for life. I was scared of what she thought about me for so long.

That evening after our talk, Stella and I went outside to sit on the front stoop of our brick Tudor home to stare at the stars. That's been one of our favorite pastimes since Stella was a toddler. We have been mapping out constellations in the sky since Stella could say "star." When she was in kindergarten, we downloaded a star tracker app on my iPhone so she could see the constellations in real time. I've always loved astronomy, and I would always tell Stella Heaven is right behind those stars. I wanted her to know it's a big world with so much to explore.

Coincidentally, Stella's full name—Estella—also means star. Stars hold great significance for all of us and have been guides for humans throughout history, even in different religions and cultures. My mother knew how much Stella and I loved the stars. When Stella and I moved into our home after living at my parents' house, my mom helped us pack up our belongings. She grabbed one of the glow-in-the-dark stars from my childhood bedroom and handed it to me. "Don't you want a star for Stella?" my mother asked me. "She can put it in her room so she can have big dreams like her mama."

I smiled and grabbed it from her. As soon as Stella got into her new bedroom, she stuck the star to her wall.

What a full-circle moment to have my daughter look up to me, even after my failures and everything we had been through. Stella deserves the unbroken version of me, and she's the reason for my healing journey. Stella deserves a mother who doesn't give up—a guiding light and leader. Stella deserves a star who will light the way and show her what's possible.

Real change can happen, but you have to visualize it and believe in it. My sobriety has given me new life. I know myself better now than I ever have. What happened to me can be my power.

Most importantly, sobriety taught me so much about self-love. Living alcohol-free, in my opinion, is the highest form of self-love. I hated my past and what I had been through, but I knew the only thing that was going to fix my life was loving myself.

It's empowering to know I can show up for Stella at any time and alcohol will never stand in the way again. Often when Stella would come home from being with her dad, I had no energy to play with her because I was hungover. I felt worthless as a mother, and I am so grateful I never have to feel that way *ever again.*

Healing my trauma through psychotherapy with Dr. Stormberg has helped me forgive myself and the woman I used to be. That binge-drinking woman was hurting, but now she's healing. Dr. Stormberg told me not to regret any of the journey because every piece of it was necessary for where I am today, and he reminded me, "All of these events had to happen in your life to move you forward. Never forget that."

CHAPTER 15

A NEW NORMAL

Not only was I healing, but Jesse was experiencing his own growth, too. Out of nowhere, it was like I was co-parenting with a completely different person. After years of constant bickering and disagreeing about literally everything when it came to Stella, we were finally getting along. He was not objecting to my requests any longer, we were agreeing on things, and we were even communicating like friends.

It was the summer of 2020 when I really started to notice a difference in him. Maybe living through a global pandemic was helping him see the bigger picture and understand we needed to be healthy and happy for our daughter and set an example for her. We both had lost someone we knew to COVID-19, and I think that also opened his eyes a bit. Life is short, and we all deserve to be happy—especially our Stella.

I had a good feeling things were going to be different from here on out. Maybe there was a bright side of the pandemic. We had a new appreciation for one another; it was our new normal.

I was so happy and relieved. I had been praying for years and years to be able to co-parent with him and get along for our daughter so she could still have the best life possible, even if her parents were no longer married. The knowledge always weighed on me that my daughter had to grow up with divorced parents, but now that we were getting along, I could see a difference in Stella, too. Her spirits were lifted, and she was comfortable talking to me in front of her dad and vice versa.

In May of 2021, Jesse actually celebrated *me* being the mother of his child. In a text to me, he wrote:

"Happy Mother's Day. Thank you for being a great mom to my princess."

I didn't know a text message could make me so emotional until I got that one. I bawled my eyes out. God again was coming through for me. God was showing me that regardless of the years of pain we had inflicted on each other through a failing marriage, divorce, and a custody fight, we could still be great role models—together—for our daughter.

That was the first time in six years Jesse actually praised me for my parenting. Talk about a complete turnaround from the Jesse who had so much animosity toward me for so long.

In the past, I would send him a "Happy Father's Day" text message, and the only response I would get from him was:

"Don't text me unless it's about Stella!"

I had so much peace in my heart. My friends and family could see the difference in me, too. I was more relaxed, and I actually talked about Jesse in a positive light. That made them suspicious.

"Do not go there!" I would tell my family and friends. "I am not getting back with Jesse. We are just co-parenting well, and I'm really proud of us!"

Dating wasn't on my radar at all for a long time after my divorce. I knew I had a lot of internal work to focus on and that was my priority. My friends had tried to get me to sign up for dating apps like Bumble and Tinder, but I refused. I stayed focused on graduate school, my own healing, and being the best mom I could. I knew rushing into a relationship wouldn't be healthy for me or Stella.

I have to admit, I was also a little afraid to put myself out there and date again. I had never been in a healthy relationship, and I didn't feel I had worked on myself enough to heal and be ready for a serious relationship. I also wasn't ready to bring someone new around my daughter. After everything we had been through, I wanted to give Stella stability and focus on building our relationship as mother and daughter. I valued our time together much more now because I knew what it was like to lose custody and miss out on valuable time with her. Giving her all of me was the best decision I could ever make. Stella was doing remarkably well. She had straight A's, was advancing quickly in her piano lessons, and most importantly, she was happy.

Jesse and I decided to surprise Stella with a trip to New York City for her tenth birthday. Stella was stoked when she found out she was going to the Big Apple for her birthday with both her mother and her father.

Seeing her so excited as we boarded the plane was such a joy for me. I watched her stare out the window of the airplane as we took off, giddy and full of bliss. Making silly faces and wiggling around in her seat, she literally couldn't sit still for the entire two-hour flight.

I calmly sat on the airplane. I had nothing to worry about in that moment. I was proud of my growth and proud of my ability to forgive Jesse and put my feelings of anger and resentment toward him behind me. I was proud of Jesse for his growth, too. Talk about a 180-degree turn from that airplane ride home nearly six years before when I first found out Jesse had filed for divorce.

I can't help but think of the irony of being high up in the sky, closer to the stars and closer to Heaven. Was that a coincidence? Not to me. I was high in the sky when I was at my lowest point and high in the sky when I felt so much peace about who I was and where my life was headed. The fact Jesse and I could co-parent like champions and give this birthday trip to Stella was a miracle, *really*. God just kept showing up to prove how great and powerful He can be.

Jesse and I were able to talk, look each other in the eyes, and act like adults the entire trip. We both had come so far. It was priceless for me to know we could be there for our daughter. It was all for Stella, who deserved this. She needed both of her parents to pour into her, and she never looked happier. God is good.

It was a beautiful feeling to know I could make mistakes and not just recover but come back stronger and thrive. I was no longer ashamed of my story or what struggles I had to overcome. I knew God had led me down this path. He wanted me to discover my purpose: to share my story, give others hope, and show the world anything is possible when you have faith and believe in yourself.

* *

I stood on the observation deck at the top of the Empire State Building and looked out over the big city. I couldn't help but sing the Alicia Keys chorus from "Empire State of Mind" in my head. She was spot on. I felt inspired by the big city lights, and I felt like a new person ready to accomplish so many things as I walked those New York City streets with Stella and her father.

I felt like everything was working out perfectly for the first time in my post-divorce life. All my stars were aligning. I was happier and a better mother. I was more present, and I valued our family time more than ever.

With every obstacle, every failure, and every heartache, I've learned there will always be some sort of benefit. There will always be a bright side to the darkness. For me, I've learned so many incredible lessons, including who I truly am. I would not be who I am today without my challenges and struggles. Had Jesse not filed for divorce, I don't know that I would have ever changed my habits or uncovered what was holding me back.

I've realized life can be amazing, even with its turbulence and traumas. You get to change. You get to choose who you want to be, and every day is a new opportunity to be your best self.

CONCLUSION

In 2010, I ran my first full marathon—26.2 miles—in Madison, Wisconsin. I trained daily for twenty weeks, incorporating mobility and yoga on non-running days. It was grueling, and I loved it. Race day brought many unexpected challenges such as a much hillier course than expected and a dangerous heat index that eventually forced organizers to stop the race. Runners were facing heat exhaustion and dehydration. We were told by race organizers if we wanted to keep running, we were doing it at our own risk. Vans were available to take us back to the starting line if we couldn't take the heat any longer. Give up and get in the van, or keep pushing forward, carefully and with a lot of water? I had already passed the halfway point, so I kept running.

I walked when I had to and stayed cool thanks to homeowners along the course who were spraying runners with hoses. I just kept moving and *focusing on one step at a time.*

I can't help but compare writing this book to running my first marathon. Both contained so many unknowns, they are mentally and emotionally challenging, and you often think about giving up. I had to stay focused on one sentence at a time. I finally crossed the Madison Marathon finish line after five and a half hours of straight determination. As I am writing this conclusion, I am nearing the finish line for *A Star for Stella*, too. It's been far from easy, but it was worth it.

I needed to write this book for myself. I wanted to prove to myself I'm capable of accomplishing all of my dreams and checking even the most difficult goals off my bucket list.

Sobriety is the best thing I could have ever done for myself. I broke generational curses and discovered how alcohol negatively impacted my life and held me back for years.

Leia and her daughter Stella pose during a photoshoot in October 2020. Photo by Ginnie Coleman Photography.

When I decided to live sober, I had no idea that would mean a promotion in my job, improved relationships, completely paying off credit card debt, publishing my first book, starting my own speaking business, and landing my highest-paid speaking gig.

If you're reading this, I appreciate you so much! Thank you for going on this journey with me where I can authentically be myself without worry, shame, or embarrassment.

I truly believe what's meant to be will always be, and this book is a perfect example of that. Prayer works, and God hears our hearts. In the middle of a global pandemic when everyone in my hometown of Omaha, Nebraska, was on a lockdown due to the coronavirus, I decided to use the time stuck in my house creatively. I started jotting down ideas for a book and began crafting my thoughts. On September 25, 2020, I finished the first chapter! I had no idea how to publish a book, so I Googled it—and that's probably the worst thing I could have done. I was overwhelmed with information about publishers and literary agents and self-publishing. It was too much information, so I left it alone. I prayed on it and trusted God would bring me to it when it was my time and if it was meant for me.

A few months later, I received a random Facebook message from one of my high school volleyball coaches. She wanted me to meet one of her friends who was writing a book about bravery and looking for inspiring stories to include in her book. After her author friend interviewed me, I asked for advice on the publishing process because I wanted to write a book, but I had no idea where to start. She connected me with the Creator Institute and New Degree Press, and here I am. If that's not God's work, I don't know what is. That is just too good to be a coincidence.

Writing this book has been extremely cathartic for me. I hope it has helped you to see how good things can happen, even after terrible situations or traumas. I hope *A Star for Stella* showed you how we can still have peace, success, and happiness, even after we fail and make mistakes. When we have the courage to face whatever is holding us back and we refuse to give up, we become unstoppable.

In the moments I felt like I was breaking, I was actually building. I was gearing up for a journey to find myself, to uncover unhealed traumas, and do the necessary work—the hard work—to live my best life as the best version of myself. I was working not only for me, but for Stella, too. Stella needed a guiding light, a powerful force to shine bright even in the darkest times, a strong and determined role model and a loving mama who could always show up at her best. Stella needed a star, and I'm grateful to God I get to be hers.

ACKNOWLEDGMENTS

———

I truly believe we rise by lifting others, and I personally want to thank each and every one of you—my readers—for investing in my journey and supporting my dream of becoming an author. This would not have been possible without my dream team of campaign supporters who pre-ordered *A Star for Stella*, shared my campaign on social media, and helped me exceed my goal. Thank you for believing in me:

Adam Kucirek, Aileen Lopez, Aileen Beyer, A'Jamal Byndon, Alejandra Jimenez, Alejandra Sinecio, Alexa Hernandez, Alina Lopez, Alisa Rangel, Alisha Madej, Alyssa LeGrand, Alyssia Salvo, Amanda Simonson, Amber Richardson, Amelia Onate, Amy Begley, Amy Lopez, Amy Onate, Anadelia Morgan, Andrea Clark, Andrea Hilario, Angela Griffith, Angi Sada, Ann Martinez, Anna Hernández, Anna Ripley, Anna Vargas, April Bishop, April Kielion, April Taylor, Ashley Kruse, Beatriz Gonzalez, Becky App, Beth Barker, Bi Nguyen, Bianca Bautista, Blas Hilario Jr., Brad Benson, Brenda Duran, Brian Clark, Brianne Schuler, Brooke Janousek, Candance Rocha, Carla Rizzo, Carol & Joe Clark, Carrie Beach Stika, Cassandra Rey, Catherene Bilek, Cathie de Loa, Cathy Saligheh, Cecilia Gulizia, Celia Remijio, Chagdrick Berger, Chelsea Correa, Chris Cantu, Christina Cloud, Christina Reyes, Cindy Bartlett Marek, Colby Barak, Constance Baughman, Cortney Companio, Courtney Clark, Cris Hay-Merchant, Crystal Rush Cardenas, Cynthia Gonzalez, Daniella Remijio-Widtfeldt, David LeRette Jr., Davina Lane, Dena Modra, Denise Allacher, Donell Deleon-Thompson, Eric Carlson, Eric Koester, Esperanza Valencia, Felicitas Remijio, Fran Hernandez, Francisco Fuentes, Georgia Lopez, Gerald Leahy, Gina Ciganek, Gina Krasnow, Ginnie Coleman, Grace Lordemann, Grace Salvo, In memory of Ysabel de Loa, Jacqueline DuPass, Jacqueline Jo Harris, Jaime Blunt, Jamalia Parker, James Valencia, Jamie Zadina, Jana Andrews, Janis Winterhof, Jeffrey Koterba, Jenni Shukert, Jennifer Clark, Jennifer Lerdahl Armstrong, Jennifer McKinney, Jennifer Prososki, Jenny Channell, Jessica Rangel, Jessica Rogat, Jill A. Martinez, Jill Holmes, Jo Zaragosa, Jody Towne, Joelle Goforth, Joey Davis, Jose Flores Jr., Jose Sanchez, Josie Loza, Juanita Deleon, Julie Holbrook, Kaitlin Breitag, Karen Cole, Karen Corral de Pesek, Karen Hicks, Karis Shaffer, Karyn Stodden, Kathy Palma, Keith Belman, Kelly Murkins, Kelly Ziola, Kim de Loa, Kimberly Isherwood, Kimi Jensen, Kristi Geho, Kristin Neumann, Krystal Hynek, Kylene Cunningham, Lamarr Womble, Lara Gale, Laura Kitzman, Laura Martinez, Laura Peters, Laura Rice, Laura Valencia, Laurie Reyes, Lee Valencia, Leslie Christensen, Letisia Perez, Linda Wilson, Lisa Cuevas-Jorgensen, Lisa Nemec-Andersen, Lisa Woodcook, Liz Hruska, Louisa Ramos, Lupe Rosas, Lydia Zaragosa, Lynette Hartin-Kovy, Lynn Pfeffer, Madison Boehme, Maggie O'Brien, Maggie O'Donnell, Margarito Gonzalez, Maria Caballero, Maria Hernandez, Maria Vazquez, Marie Claire Andrea, Mario

Juarez, Marquita Govan, Mary Ann Borgeson, Mary Brown, Mary de Loa, Mary Field, Mary Lyn Cabral, Megan Elliott, Melina Greger, Melissa Anderson, Michelle Revis, Miles Schaefer, Mimi Hannor, Mona Baez, Monica Brown, Monica Henderson, Monica Valadez, Natasha Husband, Nichole Hulstine, Nichole Olsen, Nick Juliano, Nicole Bianchi, Nicole Boyer, Nicole Danielle, Nicole Dyer, Nicole Holbrook, Nicole Morton, Nicole Wiese, Niki Linniman, Nina Newland, Olivia de Loa Castañeda, Olivia Startzer, Patrick McNary, Perri Jones, Queena Asia, Rachael Flores, Rachel Cyboron, Rachel Pacheco, Rachel Pierce, Randall Carney, Raymundo Perez, Rebecca Maher, Rick Shukert, Robin Black, Rosa Valencia, Rosalva Reyes, Rose Emery, Ruth Shukert, Selene Espinoza, Salvador Robles, Samantha Flynn, Sara Alexander, Sara Pauley, Shauna Riggs, Shelby Levy, Shirley Newson, Sonya Flores, Stefanie Monge, Stephanie Reyes, Sue Burton, Susan Benes, Susan Brown, Susan LeGrand, Tanya Shapiro, Tara Batley, Tara Chin, Terry Lee, Theresa Baez, Tim Collins, Timothy Chan, Timothy Seretta, Tina Clark, Tina Jensen-DeLeon, T.J. Ernst, Toi Hershman, Tonya McLain, Travis Harlow, Tricia Patterson, Vanessa Hoffmann, Veronica Castro, Victor Baez III, Victor Baez Jr., Victoria Lopez Parrott, Virginia Myszkowski, Yolanda Belman, and Yvonne Sosa.

APPENDIX

———

CHAPTER 9

Byrne, Rhonda. *The Secret*. New York City: Atria Books/Beyond Words, 2006.

CHAPTER 12

Klane, Robert. *Weekend at Bernie's*. Directed by Ted Kotcheff. Los Angeles, CA: Gladden Entertainment, 1989.

CHAPTER 13

Car Insurance 101. "The Drunkest Cities in America [+ Binge Drinking Stats]." Accessed November 4, 2020. https://www.carinsurance101.com/cities-with-worst-drinking-problem/.

Centers for Disease Control and Prevention. "Binge Drinking." Accessed November 4, 2020. https://www.cdc.gov/alcohol/factsheets/binge-drinking.htm.

Nebraska Department of Health and Human Services. "Nebraska Young Adult Alcohol Opinion Survey—2020." Accessed November 4, 2020. https://dhhs.ne.gov/Behavioral%20Health%20Documents/Young%20Adult%20Alcohol%20Opinion%20Survey%20State%20Report%20-%202020.pdf.

CHAPTER 14

Perry, Bruce, and Oprah Winfrey. *What Happened To You?: Conversations on Trauma, Resilience, and Healing.* New York: Flatiron Books: An Oprah Book, 2021.

Tedeschi, Richard, and Bret Moore. *The Posttraumatic Growth Workbook.* Oakland, California: New Harbinger Publications, Inc., 2016.

ABOUT THE AUTHOR

Leia Baez, author of *A Star for Stella*. Photo by Ginnie Coleman Photography.

Leia Baez is an award-winning journalist, government communications director, motivational speaker, and mindset coach based in Omaha, Nebraska. While Leia spent most of her career telling other people's stories as a journalist, it's her own story of overcoming adversity that has gone viral online, reaching more than 6.5 million people across the globe.

Read more about her journey at leiabaez.com.

Engage with her on social media at www.instagram.com/leia_baez and www.facebook.com/leiabaezspeaks.

Use #StarforStella on social media to share how Leia's story has made a difference for you.